☆ INSIGHT COMPACT GUIDE

ITALIaN RIVIeRa

Compact Guide: Italian Riviera is the ultimate quick-reference guide to this well-established, glamorous destination. It tells you all you need to know about the coast's attractions, from the the historic city of Genoa to the timeless beauty of the Cinque Terre, from bustling coastal resorts to peaceful mountain villages.

This is one of 133 Compact Guides, combining the interests and enthusiasms of two of the world's best-known information providers: Insight Guides, whose innovative titles have set the standard for visual travel guides since 1970, and Discovery Channel, the world's premier source of nonfiction television programming.

Discovery CHANNEL

APA PUBLICATIONS
Part of the Langenscheidt Publishing Group

L

Insight Compact Guide: Italian Riviera

Written by Manfred Braunger
English version by David Ingram
Updated by Adele Evans
Photography and cover picture by Mark Read
Design: Roger Williams
Picture Editor: Hilary Genin
Maps: Polyglott
Design concept: Carlotta Junger

Editorial Director: Brian Bell
Managing Editor: Tony Halliday

CONTACTING THE EDITORS: As every effort is made to provide accurate information in this publication, we would appreciate it if readers would call our attention to any errors and omissions by contacting:
Apa Publications, PO Box 7910, London SE1 1WE, England.
Fax: (44 20) 7403 0290
e-mail: insight@apaguide.co.uk

Information has been obtained from sources believed to be reliable, but its accuracy and completeness, and the opinions based thereon, are not guaranteed.

© 2006 APA Publications GmbH & Co. Verlag KG Singapore Branch, Singapore.

First Edition 1996, Second Edition 2002, Updated 2006
Printed in Singapore by Insight Print Services (Pte) Ltd
Original edition © Polyglott-Verlag Dr Bolte KG, Munich

Worldwide distribution enquiries:
APA Publications GmbH & Co. Verlag KG (Singapore Branch)
38 Joo Koon Road, Singapore 628990
Tel: (65) 6865 1600, Fax: (65) 6861 6438

Distributed in the UK & Ireland by:
GeoCenter International Ltd
The Viables Centre, Harrow Way, Basingstoke,
Hampshire RG22 4BJ
Tel: (44 1256) 817 987, Fax: (44 1256) 817 988

Distributed in the United States by:
Langenscheidt Publishers, Inc.
36–36 33rd Street 4th Floor, Long Island City, NY 11106
Fax: 1 (718) 784 0640

www.insightguides.com

Introduction

Places

Culture

Travel Tips

◁ **Genoa (p22)**
The capital of Liguria has a rumbustious maritime history and is one of the largest Old Towns in Europe. With galleries and grand palaces, it has a huge array of architectural and artistic masterpieces to enjoy.

▷ **Albenga (p74)**
Amongst the fine medieval architecture of this beautiful town are high towers and old palazzi.

▷ **La Spezia (p55)**
Fascinating artefacts in the region's naval city include Bronze Age stelae.

◁ **Finalborgo (p71)**
The 15th-century heart of this delightful town is almost completely intact.

▷ **San Remo (p88)**
Queen of the Riviera's resorts, San Remo has been attracting visitors for 150 years.

◁ **Portofino (p42)**
This former fishing village is the most fashionable spot on the Riviera – and also one of the prettiest.

△ **La Brigue frescoes (p102)** Unique in the Alps are the 15th century fresco cycles in La Brigue's pilgrimage church.

△**Cinque Terre (p48)** Remote and timeless, the communities of the 'five lands' are the quintessential Riviera, where mountains come down to the sea.

△**Dolceacqua (p95)** Claude Monet was one of the first visitors to this mountain town, and today its medieval bridge is often photographed.

▷ **Lavagna (p47)** This 13th century basilica is one of the best examples of Romanesque-Gothic architecture in Liguria.

A Classic Coastline

The Italian Riviera: the name conjures up images of palm trees and cacti, thick *macchia* and vast fields of cloves, of elegant hotels and suntanned millionaires. The Riviera certainly is all that – a lush and fragrant sunny region between the mountains and the sea. But the three million or so visitors who come here each year are attracted not only by its endless meadows of flowers and its beautiful coastline, but also by its thousands of years of history and its cultural legacy. Among the region's famous sons, both born in the capital, Genoa, are the explorer Christopher Columbus (1451) and the virtuoso violinist Nicolò Paganini (1782).

Genoa has been unjustly neglected for some time now. It was much praised by travellers of previous centuries, especially the French novelist Gustave Flaubert who, in 1845, referred to it enthusiastically as 'a city built entirely of marble, with gardens full of roses, and a beauty which tears at the soul'.

The resorts of Bordighera and San Remo are rather like elderly ladies accustomed to better times, but both have adapted to the exigencies of modern tourism; Portofino does its best to shield its VIPs from over-curious eyes; Alassio revolves entirely around entertainment; Albenga exudes a medieval atmosphere; and the ever popular villages that make up the coastal jewel of the Cinque Terre have accepted a moderate amount of tourism, in order to save their dizzyingly steep vineyard terraces from destruction by roads and motorways.

LIGURIA'S TWO FACES

The Ligurian Mediterranean coast also has a less attractive side, however. Alongside the breathtaking *bellezza* there are also the problems faced by Genoa's Old Town, in the traffic-choked Via Aurelia, and among the faceless concrete highrise apartment blocks surrounding many of the resorts. These scars have by and large been

Contradictions
'So lively, and yet so dead: so noisy, and yet so quiet; so obtrusive and yet so shy and lowering; so wide awake, and yet so fast asleep; that it is a sort of intoxication to a stranger to walk on, and on, and look about him.' Charles Dickens writing on Liguria in *Pictures from Italy*, 1846.

Left: the beach at Alassio
Below: a local farmer
Bottom: street shrine, Altare

hidden by the Riviera's ever fascinating natural scenery, by its perfectly organised beach resorts and by its picturesque mountain villages. So far, anyway.

The Italian Riviera is the coastal strip of Liguria, an ancient province, and a well known vine and olive-growing area. It has two faces: the resorts along the coast, which extend like a string of pearls from Bordighera in the west to the Cinque Terre in the east, and the region inland. As a continuation of the French Riviera, which it meets at the border at Ventimiglia, the holiday coast has been marketed as the Italian Riviera for the past 150 years. (Northern Europeans used to consider bathing an Italian perversity and the vogue for swimming did not really take off until the 1930s.)

The Riviera comprises not only the highly-regarded resorts, such as San Remo and Portofino, where thousands of sunbathers gather, but also the peaceful mountain villages further inland, often only a few miles from the sea, where time seems to have stood still.

Liguria is relatively small – a narrow strip of land squeezed in between the mountains and the sea. The luxuriant Mediterranean vegetation along the coast contrasts vividly with the stark and severe mountain scenery higher up, and the Ligurians down on the coast, who have lived off seafaring and fishing for centuries, seem to have little in common with their compatriots in the mountains, who grow produce as best they can on the often barren soil.

Time stands still in the mountain villages

POSITION AND SIZE

Liguria has a total surface area of just 5,418sq km (2,090sq miles), making it the third smallest region in Italy after the Molise and the Val d'Aosta. It ranges from 7.5km (4½ miles) to 38km (23 miles) in width, and is roughly 275km (170 miles) long, extending around the Gulf of Genoa, the northernmost part of the Ligurian Sea. The mountains and hills form the Regione

Liguria, accurately described in the tourist brochures as a colourful mix of the Alps and the Apennines; the point where the two mighty mountain ranges meet is generally considered to be the 465-m (1,525-ft) Cole di Cadibona near Savona. The highest peak in Liguria is Monte Saccarello (2,200m/7,217ft), which lies in the Western Alps, on the Franco-Italian border.

Below: Apricale clings to the slopes
Bottom: Camogli harbour

MOUNTAIN AND SEA

The narrow coastal strip connects with a series of mountain valleys, most of them quite short. Within the space of just a few miles they rise steeply from the Mediterranean climatic zone, with its palm trees, olive groves and vineyards, into the Alpine zone, full of beech, larch and pine, creating the sharp contrast in landscape for which Liguria is so well-known. The proximity of the mountains to the coast creates climatic extremes: the Mediterranean southern slopes are right next to the kind of scenery more often associated with Central or Northern Europe.

The streams that pour down the mountainsides and through the valleys can often burst their banks and become raging torrents; this has happened increasingly often in recent years, and many rivers and streams are now bordered by concrete walls to allow the water to crash down into the valleys

unhindered. Mountain slopes which used to absorb much of the rainwater have been built on and concreted over by urban development, resulting in disastrous flooding of streets and cellars – not only in Genoa itself but many other coastal resorts as well.

Landslides are also a common problem in Liguria; anyone driving inland after a period of heavy rain should check with the authorities beforehand to see which mountain routes are still passable.

Steep slopes
There is such a short distance between the sea and the mountains in Liguria that it has a higher percentage of mountains than any other region in Italy.

Below: Monte di Portofino Nature Reserve
Bottom: slate quarry, Valle di Fontanabuona

GEOLOGY

Liguria's fragile geological equilibrium can be traced to the fact that the region is composed primarily of soft sandstone and marl, formed during the Cretaceous Period (65–130 million years ago) and extending across the whole of western Liguria, as well as a large area to the east of Genoa. The Apennine peaks behind Genoa and Savona consist of various kinds of serpentine stone. Most striking is the green serpentine stone, without which the fascinating light-and-dark effect of many Ligurian churches and palazzi would be unthinkable.

One classic serpentine mountain is Monte Beigua *(see page 63)*. Also fascinating geologically is the limestone region, formed between 200 and 250 million years ago, which characterises

the mountain landscape between Albenga and Savona; it is a paradise for climbers and potholers alike.

Inland from Finale Ligure and also near Toirano and Ventimiglia, several limestone caverns formerly inhabited by the earliest Ligurians are now open to tourists.

Apart from serpentine and marble (famous examples include *portoro* from Portofino, the red-and-green marble from Levanto and green marble from Pegli), slate has long been a popular construction material in Liguria. There are still slate quarries today in the Valle Fontanabuona near Lavagna, and many of the houses in Ligurian villages still have delightful slate portals.

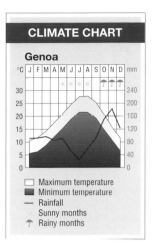

CLIMATE CHART

Genoa

☐ Maximum temperature
■ Minimum temperature
— Rainfall
Sunny months
☂ Rainy months

CLIMATE AND WHEN TO GO

It was the mild and temperate climate which attracted (predominantly English) tourists to the Italian Riviera in the middle of the 19th century. Unlike today's visitors who occupy the Ligurian beaches from late spring to early autumn, they came to spend the winter here; unsurprisingly, in view of the mild climate.

The average winter temperatures along the coast seldom sink below 8°C (46°F), and are as high as 10°C (50°F) between Alassio and San Remo – something only experienced again down at the Gulf of Naples. The summer temperatures are also very bearable thanks to a fresh sea breeze, averaging between 22°C (71°C) and 24°C (75°C). Snow falls in Genoa on an average of two days a year, and two to six days in La Spezia. The months with the lowest rainfall are July and August.

Liguria is a great place to visit all year round. Those in search of warms seas and a tan will opt for the summer months; visitors in search of culture and history tend to visit the region in spring and autumn, when the roads are less full and the hotels and campsites have space again. And in spring there is the bonus of colourful flowers. Or why not visit in winter – just as the English did in the mid-19th century?

Sunny resident, Pievo di Teco

Sun up, sun down
Eastern Liguria is known as the Levante – a reference to the rising sun. After the area around Genoa, the western side of Liguria is called Ponente – a reference to where the sun sets.

Below: botanical gardens in Ventimiglia
Bottom: vineyard in Comiglia

Nature and the Environment

Liguria has 13 nature reserves, made up of 10 regional parks *(Parchi naturali regionali)* and three regional reserves *(Riserve naturali regionali)*. Among the finest of the regional reserves is the Isola Gallinara, an 11-hectare (27-acre) island in the province of Savona. Only a few miles away from the heavily built-up coast, it shows what the flora in the region looked like before the advent of tourism. Boats take tourists around the privately-owned island.

The Rio Torsero nature reserve, encompassing 4 hectares (9 acres) and also located in the province of Savona, is famous for its astonishingly well-preserved fossils from the Pliocene Era (5.2–1.3 million years ago).

Inland from Chiavari in the province of Genoa, the Aveto nature reserve (10,380 hectares/25,650 acres) contains several lakes which date from the Ice Age and the rich flora which is typical of marshland areas.

The Monte di Portofino nature reserve (4,650 hectares/11,500 acres) in Santa Maria Lighure is a real highlight of any trip to Liguria, with its scenic beauty and cultural sights such as the monastery of San Fruttuoso *(see page 41)* – and the same goes for the five famous villages that make up the Cinque Terre *(see page 48)*, which are protected by the nature reserve that also includes Montemarcello.

The land produces healthy food and some of the best olive oil in Italy; the Museo dell'Olivo *(see page 82)* documents the vital contribution of the humble olive to the region's history.

The Coast

The 317-km (197-mile) Riviera coast is a sight in itself; mostly rocky, it has preserved its original character in only a few areas. However, bathers can rest assured that in recent years only around 3 percent of the Ligurian beaches have been off-limits because of pollution (Tuscany and the Northern Adriatic were the only places to score better), though it should be borne in mind that towns along the Western Riviera *(Riviera di*

Ponente, comprising the provinces of Savona and Imperia) outdid their Eastern Riviera *(Riviera di Levante)* counterparts such as Genoa and La Spezia, whose harbours have caused quite a bit of pollution.

Liguria has more forests than any other part of Italy: they cover 53 percent of its surface. Since much of the woodland faces south, forest fires are quite common.

POPULATION

Liguria has a population of roughly 1.56 million, of whom some 605,000 live in the capital, Genoa. The population density is far above Italy's average, even though the number of inhabitants overall has been gradually decreasing over the past few years. Most of the population lives along the narrow coastal strip. New job opportunities in industry, and especially in tourism, are leading to a gradual depopulation of the remote mountain regions. The empty houses and often completely deserted villages provide accommodation for northern and central Europeans weary of civilisation, and also for Italians from neighbouring regions who have found a second home here, either for a few months a year or permanently.

Ligurians, long a nation of traders, are said to be pugnacious, resourceful and enterprising.

Below: soaking up the sun
Bottom: beach life

Andrea Doria

In Italian history books, Andrea Doria is praised as the hero who saved Liguria. In reality, he was a clever and capricious mercenary leader, who made a series of skilful political moves to rule Genoa for 30 years. Born in 1466 in Oneglia, Andrea Doria embarked on a military career in the service of Pope Innocent VIII, the Neapolitan kings Ferdinand I and Alphonse II, and the Borgias' rival Giovanni della Rovere. He fought against an uprising on Corsica, was universally feared by pirates, ran a used-ship business, defeated the papal-imperial fleet that tried to conquer Genoa, and placed his vessels at the service of François I of France. Together with his cousin, Filippino, he defeated Emperor Charles V's fleet, but a few weeks later he changed sides and entered the Emperor's service. With Charles V's support he became the ruler, or 'Doge', of Genoa, controlling the city's fortunes until his death in 1569.

La Spezia harbour

LANGUAGE

Even Italian speakers can be forgiven for not understanding much of what is spoken along the Riviera. Ligurian is one of the Northern Italian dialects, and is really hard to understand even for other Italians. Its distinctive features include a tendency to contract various sounds, miss out consonants between vowels and alter the sound of long 'o' s and 'a's. For instance, *nuovo* (new) becomes *növu*, *nuora* (daughter-in-law) becomes *nöa*, and *cuore* (heart) is contracted down to *cö*. Place names tend to be noticeably different from the official ones: Genoa is known to the locals as *Sena*, Savona as *Sana*, Rovereto as *Ruveóu*, and Arenzano as *Aensén*.

The list could be continued indefinitely – all the way to San Remo, which was first known as *San Romolo* and then changed into the local dialect version *San Römu*, before finally being 'translated' into written Italian as San Remo.

ECONOMY

In terms of per capita income, Liguria is the third-wealthiest Italian region after the Val d'Aosta and Lombardy. Tourism is doubtless one of the main reasons for this relative prosperity: the Riviera is the most popular region of Italy for the tourist trade. Here again the double face of Liguria becomes

apparent: 80 percent of tourism in the region is along the coast, and just 20 percent further inland.

Iron, steel, engineering, petrochemicals and shipbuilding are cornerstones of local industry, as is olive oil production. The Ligurian harbours turn over a record amount of goods. Genoa is the most important harbour in the country, and as a passenger port only third in importance to Brindisi and Venice. Along with La Spezia and Savona (Italy's export harbour for Fiat and Lancia cars), Genoa handles one fifth of Italian passenger traffic and one sixth of its goods traffic.

Along the Western Riviera, flower cultivation is a very important industry, accounting for 50 percent of national production, and the innumerable glasshouses are a distinctive feature of the landscape, giving the coast the name of Riviera dei Fiori (Riviera of the Flowers). Although only a small proportion of the wine produced in the region is exported, viticulture is also a factor in the local economy, with three Ligurian wines having a DOC, the government mark of quality.

As far as arts and crafts are concerned, there are ceramics from Albisola, bells from Avegno, filigree jewellery from Campo Ligure, chairs from Chiavari, velvet from Zoagli, brocade and damask from Lorsica, bobbin lace from Portofino, Santa Margherita Ligure, Paraggi and Camogli, glass from Altare, church clocks from Recco, Uscio and Pietra Ligure, toys from the Valle Fontanabuona, and lavender from Pietrabruna.

POLITICS AND ADMINISTRATION

Liguria, officially the *Regione Liguria*, is one of Italy's 20 regions. Its capital is Genoa (Italian *Genova*), and Liguria is divided up into the four provinces of Genoa, Imperia, La Spezia and Savona. Mayors are elected and have a degree of power. Politically, the Italian regions are anything but federal; their statutes allow for no independent decision-making. Though the system is far from feudal, most of the regions are still very much under the control of the central government in Rome.

Below: produce from the Riviera dei Fiori
Bottom: Genoese sailor

HISTORICAL HIGHLIGHTS

Palaeolithic Period Traces of human habitation in caves, up to 300,000 years old.

Bronze Age Thousands of cave paintings appear in the Vallée des Merveilles.

6th century BC The Ligurians are driven out of the Po Plain by invading Gauls. Some settle in today's Liguria, mixing with the local tribes and becoming fishermen and coastal traders.

5th century BC Genoa is a sizable metropolis, trading with Greeks and Etruscans.

180BC Roman conquest of Liguria, bringing prosperity with Roman naval bases.

5th–6th centuries After the fall of the Roman Empire, Genoa and smaller ports such as La Spezia and Savona continue to develop as trading ports.

641 Genoa is conquered by King Rothan of Lombardy.

936 Genoa is destroyed by the Saracens.

10th century Liguria is divided up into three marches by Berengar III.

11th–12th centuries After defeating the Saracens in 1148, Genoa begins to assert itself as the dominant power in the Mediterranean. The Crusades and trade with the Orient bring untold prosperity. As the old feudal structure weakens, the main towns in the region all assert their independence.

1284 Genoa defeats its arch rival Pisa at Meloria, a naval battle off Livorno. By the end of the 13th century, Genoa has possessions and trading posts as far afield as Constantinople and Syria; the population reaches more than 100,000, making it one of the largest cities in Europe.

14th century Genoa is racked by internal power struggles between patrician families supporting the pope (Guelphs) and the Holy Roman Emperor (Ghibellines). Despite this, the feuding families amass fortunes, and build magnificent palaces in Genoa and along the coast. There are constant rebellions by other towns against Genoese hegemony. Economic rivalry leads to increased fragmentation, and there is a return to feudalism. Local nobles create their own fiefdoms protected by hilltop castles along the coast. Towns are heavily fortified.

1339 After a series of invasions by the French and others, Simon Boccanegra is elected the first 'doge' (leader) of Genoa.

1346–8 Liguria is ravaged by the Black Death.

1378–81 Genoa is soundly defeated by Venice in the Chioggia War, signalling the end of its maritime supremacy.

Early 15th century Genoese merchants create the Banco di San Giorgio, a solid foundation for the development of the city into a world financial centre.

1451 Birth of Christopher Columbus, Genoa's most famous son.

1522 Genoa is sacked by the Spanish.

1528 Andrea Doria *(see page 14)* liberates Genoa from French dominion and rules the city single-handedly for 30 years.

mid-16th century Genoa becomes the world's leading financial city. The Spanish kings raise money here for their New World campaigns.

1576 Genoa receives a republican constitution.

1608 Genoa assumes a free port status.

17th century The Genoese lose their position as head of international banking.

1684 The French bombard and enter Genoa without encountering resistance.

1746 Liguria is occupied by Austrians, who impose an oppressive regime before being driven out by popular resistance.

1796 The aristocratic Genoese Republic is conquered by French revolutionary troops under Napoleon Bonaparte, and transformed into the French-controlled 'Ligurian Republic'.

1805 The Ligurian Republic becomes a part of France.

1815 After the downfall of Napoleon, Liguria is made over to the Kingdom of Piedmont-Sardinia as the 'Duchy of Genoa'.

After 1815 Genoa is a centre of political activism in the Italian freedom struggle.

1821–34 Three anti-Piedmontese uprisings by the Ligurians are crushed.

1849–59 Ligurian freedom-fighters Giuseppe Mazzini, Giuseppe Garibaldi, Goffredo Mameli and Nino Bixio lead the *Risorgimento* (movement for Italian independence).

1860 Garibaldi sets sail to overthrow the Bourbon dynasty ruling Sicily and southern Italy. Nice and the region surrounding it are ceded to France.

1861 Liguria becomes part of the new Kingdom of Italy under Vittorio Emanuele II.

1887 An earthquake causes serious damage in Western Liguria.

1915 Italy enters World War I on the side of Britain and France, holding the front in the Dolomites.

1922 onwards Genoa becomes a major centre of resistance to Mussolini and the forces of fascism that have enveloped the country. The movement becomes more hostile after Italy enters World War II on the side of Germany in 1940.

1943 The resistance movement manages to rescue Genoa's shipyards and other industrial installations from destruction by the German army.

1945 In April, the resistance launches a successful uprising in advance of the country's liberation by the Allies.

1947 On 10 February, the central and upper parts of the Roia Valley as far as the Colle di Tenda are ceded to France, under the terms of the Treaty of Paris.

1945 onwards Badly damaged during the war, Genoa is rebuilt and emerges as Italy's leading seaport, making a significant contribution to the postwar economic recovery. New prosperity along the Riviera comes with tourism.

1992 The Riviera coast and regions inland begin to suffer serious and recurrent flooding. The great Columbus exhibition breathes new life into the old port area of Genoa.

1999 The Cinque Terre National Park is created.

2001 Genoa hosts the June G8 Summit under maximum security. Police are heavily criticised for their over-reaction and killing of a protestor.

2004 Genoa is the European Cultural Capital. Restoration and renovation of the dockyard and Via Garibaldi.

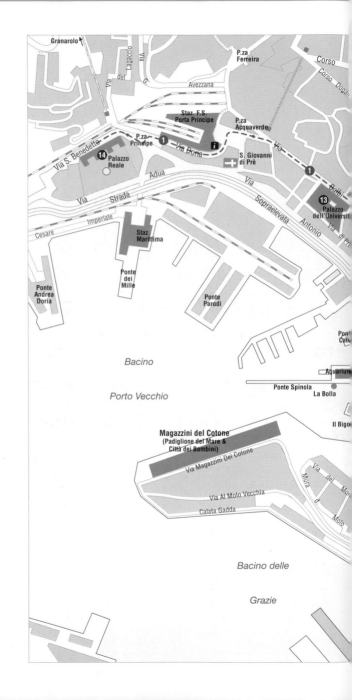

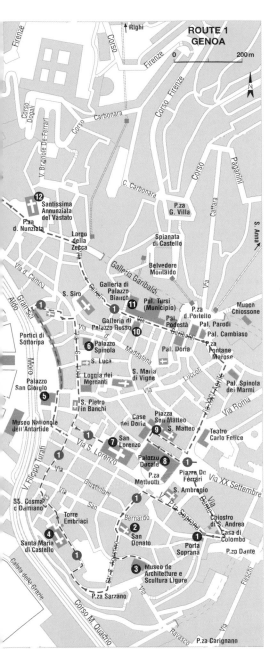

ROUTE 1
GENOA

0   200m

↑ Righi

Preceding page: Portofino
Below: Gallery Neptune
Bottom: the ubiquitous Vespa

Map
on pages
20–21

Below: Old Town café
Bottom: port panorama

1: Genoa

Genoa is not an 'easy' city from the tourist point of view. Instead of displaying its treasures proudly, it hides them away behind dark palazzo facades and traffic-ridden streets. The Genoese have always jealously guarded their privacy and, rather than attract tourists, they have largely preferred to divert them away to the Riviera resorts. As European City of Culture in 2004, the city has undergone a dramatic facelift. Baroque facades have been revealed in all their glory, especially in the Via Garabaldi, the street of some of the finest palaces in Italy. The old port has been transformed and a new Maritime Museum gives a fascinating insight into sea exploration from Genoa, the birthplace of Christopher Columbus.

HISTORY

The Ligurians who lived here before the Romans arrived traded from this natural harbour with Greeks, Etruscans, Phoenicians and Celts – and the Romans themselves, to whom Genoa lent its heartfelt support during the Punic Wars, knew just how strategically important the town was. After periods of Ostrogoth, Byzantine, Lombard and Frankish rule, Genoa began to get more self-confident. It defied the Saracens, and dared confront

the pirates on the high seas. The Genoese merchants and mariners seemed to like the sea: they took part in the Crusades, founded trading posts in the Orient and brought large amounts of booty, including the mortal relics of John the Baptist, back to their homeland. Rivalry with Pisa came to a head with the latter's defeat at sea in 1284, at the Battle of Meloria off Livorno, and Genoa also beat the Venetians (initially at least) in a battle fought close to the Dalmatian island of Curzola. Genoa had possessions and trading posts in Constantinople, the Black Sea, Armenia and Syria; it owned Corsica and part of Sardinia; it had harbours and storage depots in North Africa. By 1300, Genoa was one of the world's major powers.

> **Proud city**
> The salty capital of Liguria is Italy's sixth largest city and still basks in the glory of its noble nickname, La Superba (The Proud). It is also known as the 'City of the Lantern', a reference to the Lanterna lighthouse, which, though no longer the tallest structure, remains the symbol of the city.

STRUGGLE AND STRIFE

However, instead of enjoying their newfound wealth in peace, the city's principal families began to argue among themselves: the Fieschi, Grimaldi, Guarchi and Montalto fought against the Doria, Spinola, Adorno and Fregoso families. Genoa was threatened by the Aragonese, and subsequently conquered by Venice; it was then forced to submit to the patronage of several different lords. When America was discovered, Genoa lost its importance as a maritime power and was very nearly defeated during battles between France and Spain. At this stage, however, Andrea Doria *(see page 14)* arrived on the scene. A skilful, experienced admiral, he turned his back on his lord, François I of France, and offered France's arch-enemy, Emperor Charles V, money and ships. In 1528 Genoa became an independent republic, and until the 1560s Andrea Doria was its undisputed ruler.

Port pigeons

RENAISSANCE

Even though Genoa had suffered much political damage on the world stage, it became prosperous in the 16th and 17th centuries. New churches were built, as were magnificent palaces, all of them very much in the style of the Palazzo Doria, built by its namesake. Impressive avenues were also built,

Map on pages 20–21

After dark
Most of Genoa's late-night action is on the waterfront. The Via Gramsci has plenty of 'happening' bars and colourful characters, although you'd be well advised to hang on to your wallet. The atmosphere can be menacing as well as colourful in the maze of little alleys, (caruggi) near the port, which are probably best avoided at night.

and their splendour astonished all the Europeans who visited the city. Then Genoa was once again exposed to various warring states: Savoy, France, Austria, the French again during the Napoleonic era, Britain, Austria, France yet again – until the Genoese republic was made part of Piedmont at the Congress of Vienna in 1815, and eventually became part of the new united Italy in 1860.

As the largest port in Italy, Genoa has been seen merely as a departure or transit point. However, the Columbus celebrations in 1992 gave the city a new dynamism with the beginning of the transformation of the harbour. The famous Genoese architect Renzo Piano gave the Porto Antico a thorough face-lift for the city's celebrations as European City of Culture in 2004. The city is embracing its new-found status with all the zeal of the discoverers and matchless Italian design.

THE OLD TOWN

Genoa has a large ★★★ **Old Town**, covering 4sq km (1½sq miles), and considered to be the largest in Europe. Half of its 40,000 inhabitants are from other countries: while the Italians are gradually abandoning the *carrugi* (small dark alleyways) and the uncomfortable apartments, immigrants from northern and central Africa are moving in – many illegally – to the empty houses and using

Piazza de Ferrari

them as provisional accommodation. This Old Town is the heart of Genoa, however, and has been ever since the city's *castello* hill was populated in the 6th century BC by Ligurian settlers.

PIAZZA DANTE

From the modern **Piazza de Ferrari**, the square with the most traffic in Genoa, head for the **Piazza Dante**, where the past and the present both meet: two skyscrapers built in 1940 stand opposite the so-called **Casa de Cristoforo Colombo** (open Sat and Sun 9am–noon, 3–6pm), where the explorer is supposed to have spent his childhood (the house is an 18th-century reconstruction). The adjacent 12th-century Romanesque cloister of Sant' Andrea has some impressive capitals, and beyond it is the **Porta Soprana ❶**, part of the former medieval fortifications.

SAN DONATO

On the way to the church of **San Donato ❷** (open daily 8am–noon, 3–7pm), it's worth strolling through the Old Town, where craftsmen can still be observed at work (e.g. in the Via Giustiniani); as you do so you'll realise just how much redevelopment is still needed in this area after destruction in World War II. The church of San Donato represents one well-meant but utterly disastrous attempt at restoration (1888): the architect responsible, Alfredo d'Andrade, robbed the building almost entirely of its Romanesque character. Dominated by an octagonal Romanesque belfry, the three-aisled interior contains several Roman columns. Several noteworthy works of art inside the church include a late 14th-century *Madonna and Child* by Nicolò da Voltri, and an *Adoration of the Magi* by the Dutch painter Joos van Cleve, who lived in Genoa from 1526 to 1528.

One very good example of how successfully a cloister can be transformed into a museum is the **Museo de Architettura e Scultura Ligure ❸** (open Tues–Fri 9am–7pm, Sat–Sun 10am–7pm), next to the Gothic church of Sant'Agostino. The

Star Attraction
● Genoa's Old Town

Below: Casa de Cristoforo Colombo
Bottom: Porto Soprano

Map on pages 20–21

Below: Santa Maria di Castello
Bottom: Palazzo San Giorgio

exhibits provide a good general impression of Ligurian sculpture from the 6th to the 18th centuries. Highlights among these various architectural fragments, statues, frescoes and tomb slabs taken from Genoese churches include the *Tomb of Simon Boccanegra*, the first doge of Genoa. The church of Sant'Agostino also serves a different purpose these days: it has been turned into a modern auditorium.

SANTA MARIA DI CASTELLO

Perhaps the oldest of Genoa's 20 or so churches consecrated to the Virgin Mary is the early Christian ★ **Santa Maria di Castello** ❹ (open daily 8am–noon and 3–7pm), a largely Romanesque structure, built by the so-called *Magistri Antelami* from northern Lombardy, who constructed the new harbour. The Dominican monks who now own the building had a monastery with three cloisters attached to the three-aisled church during the 15th and early 16th century. Behind the modest facade there are gardens, frescoed walkways and broad loggias with fine views of the harbour. A small museum (open daily 9am–noon and 3.30–6pm, and till 7pm Sun) also contains valuable liturgical manuscripts and incunabula.

Alongside Santa Maria di Castello is the 12th-century **Torre degli Embriaci**, the best-preserved of the 66 or so privately owned towers of 13th-

century Genoa. Even though other towers in the city had to remain under a decreed limit of 24m (79ft), the Torre Embriaci was allowed to retain its lofty 41m (134ft) because of services to the city by the Embriaci family during the Crusades.

Star Attraction
● **Aquarium**

PALAZZO SAN GIORGIO

Go along the Via Canneto il Curto (taking a detour via the Via Canneto il Lungo, with its reliefs, friezes and slate and marble portals on the noble palazzi) as far as the ★ **Palazzo San Giorgio ❺**, one of the city's major landmarks and where Marco Polo was imprisoned in 1298 after the battle of Curzola. Built as a seat of government in 1260 by Guglielmo Boccanegra, the Genoese governor at that time, it served later as a town hall and a customs house. In the early 15th century, the influential Banco di San Giorgio made the building its headquarters. Genoa's banks were powerful during the Renaissance period: they financed the wars and caprices of the Spanish Habsburg monarchy, when Charles V and Philip II controlled half the Mediterranean. On the first floor of the building, the medieval council chamber, assembly hall and the hall of the Capitano del Popolo are open to the public (open daily 1–6pm).

THE HARBOUR

The view across the **Harbour** from the Palazzo San Giorgio should not be missed. At the harbour **Expo site** is Renzo Piano and Peter Chermayeff's superb ★★ **Aquarium** (open Mon–Wed, Fri 9.30am–7.30pm, Thur 9.30am–10pm, Sat, Sun and public holidays 9.30am–8.30pm) by the Ponte Spinola. Almost 200 tanks, reproducing natural salt and fresh-water environments and 5,000 specimens of 500 aquatic species, make this the largest aquarium in Europe. Two subterranean levels contain laboratories, monitoring stations and control panels, guaranteeing the dolphins, seals, sharks and other creatures the conditions of their natural environment. The impressive new 'World of Coral' opened in May 2005.

> **Harbour tour**
> To get a good impression of everyday life in the biggest harbour in Italy, take the 45-minute harbour round-trip from the Calata Zingara. Permanently visible during the voyage past the long quays is the 117-m (380-ft) lighthouse known as the Lanterna, the symbol of the city and the world's oldest functioning lighthouse (365 steps to the top). Anyone boarding a cruise ship from the Ponte dei Mille should take time to admire the attractive art nouveau Stazione Marittima. Today it houses the Istituto Idrografico della Marina, which can provide highly detailed maps of the whole Italian coastline. (There are also whale-watching expeditions in summer, departing from Ponte Spinola.)

Il Bigo

Map
on pages
20–21

Port sites
Darsenna, formerly a dock-yard, is an entertainment and culture complex dedicated to the Sea and Adventure. The fascinating new Galata, Museo del Mare (open Tues–Sun 10am–7.30pm; Nov–Feb till 6pm), charts the history of Genoa and its maritime connections.

On the third floor of the old Cotton Warehouse, the Padiglione del Mare e della Navigazione (Pavilion of the Sea and Navigation) (open Nov–end Feb: Mon–Fri 10.30am–5.30pm, Sat–Sun & hols 10.30am–6pm; Mar–end Oct: Mon–Fri 10.30am–7pm, Sat–Sun & hols 10.30am–7.30pm; June–end Sept: Thur, Fri, Sat & Sun till 8pm) has a permanent exhibition of mercantile marine and a room dedicated to Columbus. On the first floor is Città dei Bambini (open Tues–Sun 10am–6pm), a high-tech interactive space for children aged 3 to 16.

Galleria Nazionale in the Palazzo Spinola

AROUND PORTO ANTICO

Next to the Aquarium, Renzo Piano's **La Bolla** (open Tues–Sun 9.30am–dusk), a futuristic glass and steel bubble, contains tropical plants and rare ferns. Piano's **Il Bigo** (*see page 27*), a huge crane, hauls up a revolving panoramic lift for superb views (open Tues–Sun 10am–6pm but can close earlier in winter and later in summer). The unique **Antarctic Museum** (Museo Nazionale dell'Antartide) (open daily 10.30am–6.30pm) looks at the ecosystems of the South Pole.

The Portici di Sottoripa are a mixture of old Genoese tradition and busy harbour activity. Their arcades contain tiny shops and *friggitorie* ('frying kitchens'). From the Portici, walk down one of the side streets into the Via San Luca and to the **Palazzo Spinola** ❻ (both galleries: open Tues–Sat 8.30am–7.30pm, Sun 1–8pm, ticket office closes one hour earlier), a medieval building that received its present-day appearance in 1580. Its stucco facade and richly decorated interior are typical of 16th- to 18th-century Genoese patrician houses. The building houses the ★ **Galleria Nazionale di Palazzo Spinola**, where highlights include *Justice* by Giovanni Pisano (1313), *Ecce Homo* by Antonello da Messina, a *Praying Madonna* by Joos van Cleve and *Portrait of a Young Boy* by Anthony Van Dyck. On the third and fourth floors, the Galleria Nazionale della Liguria contains a triptych by Joos van Cleve and *Portrait of Gio Carlo Doria* by Peter Paul Rubens.
.

SAN LORENZO

Genoa's patron saint is St Lawrence, the Roman archdeacon who was grilled to death in 258. Christian iconography always depicts him as a purse, and Italians from elsewhere in the country are rather fond of teasing the (ostensibly avaricious) Genoese for worshipping this particular symbol. The cathedral consecrated to the saint is ★★ **San Lorenzo** ❼ (open Mon–Sat 8am–noon and 3–7pm, Sun 8am–12.15pm), constructed in the 9th century and rebuilt during the early years of the 12th century. The San Giovanni portal on the northern side and the San Gottardo portal on the south facade both date from that time. The mighty cathedral received its present-day appearance in the 13th century, however. French architects designed the severe facade in the style of the cathedrals in Rouen and Chartres, but – like many Ligurian churches – it was also given the characteristic black-and-white stripes.

There's an uncomfortably lifelike rendition of the death of St Lawrence on the Gothic main portal, with its marble inlay, composite capitals and reliefs. Inside the cathedral, don't miss the ★ **Cappella di San Giovanni Battista** in the south aisle. Genoa's merchants were proud of having brought the remains of John the Baptist to their city in 1098, but the reliquary only found a proper home in the 15th century when Domenico and Elia Gaggini built this Renaissance chapel. The niches also contain fine statues by 16th-century Tuscan sculptor Andrea Sansovino. The **Museo del Tesoro di San Lorenzo**, in four underground chambers (open Mon–Sat 9am–noon, 3–6pm, and every first Sun of the month 3–6pm, guided tours every half hour), is rich in relics and church treasures.

AROUND THE PALACES

A tour of the palaces begins, like a tour of the Old Town, in the Piazza de Ferrari. It proves that

Star Attraction
● San Lorenzo Cathedral

Below and bottom: San Lorenzo cathedral

Map
on pages
20–21

travellers of past centuries were quite right to praise Genoa for its impressive streets and magnificent marble *palazzi*; they justly referred to it as *La Superba*, 'the proud one'.

Right on the square is the neoclassical ★ **Teatro Carlo Felice**, rebuilt just in time for the Columbus Expo in 1992, after decades of hefty debate. The opera house built by Carlo Barabino in 1827, and destroyed during World War II, has now been restored by the architect Aldo Rossi to new, modern, and not uncontroversial splendour. (Season runs from November to May. Tel: 010-589 329.)

*Below: Palazzo Ducale
door knocker*
Bottom: Piazza San Matteo

PALAZZO DUCALE

Another modernised building is the enormous ★★ **Palazzo Ducale** ❽ (shops & restaurants open daily 9am–9pm; exhibitions open Tues–Sun 9am–9pm, admission charge), today the city's Palazzo della Cultura. After ten years' restoration work, the building, formerly the seat of government of the Genoese republic, once again radiates 16th-century magnificence. Its noble inner courtyards, the frescoed chapel, the Salone del Gran Consiglio with its frescoes and stucco, the Salone del Minor Consiglio with its glorious paintings, the seven-storeyed tower and the splendid Doge's apartments have been lovingly restored, as have several adjoining rooms under the roof and in the

basement. A vast space is available for culture, commerce, craft and gastronomy, and a super-modern, vertical steel ramp designed by architect Giovanni Spalla connects the various storeys.

Star Attraction
● **Palazzo Ducale**

PIAZZA SAN MATTEO

The nearby **Piazza San Matteo** ❾ is connected with Genoa's ubiquitous Doria family *(see page 14)*. It is Genoa's most beautiful square – a jewel of medieval urban architecture. From the 12th century the influential patrician family made this square its own, and it still retains its medieval atmosphere. Martino Doria had a church of **San Matteo** built here in 1125, and today's Gothic structure was built above its foundations in 1278 as the private church of the Doria family (open daily 9am–noon & 3–6.30pm). The crypt contains the tomb of the great Andrea Doria, designed by the Mannerist sculptor Giovanni Montorsoli. Beside the church are the Palazzo di Branca Doria, the Palazzo di Domenicaccio Doria, the Palazzo Quartara (also Doria property originally) with a relief of *St George and the Dragon* by Giovanni Gagini (1475) on its portal, the Palazzo di Lamba Doria and the Palazzo di Andrea Doria, with subtle, late Gothic elements. What makes the Piazza Matteo so harmonious are the light and dark stripes running around all the buildings.

Genova Card
A three day Genova Card offers admission to most museums and free transport. Available from the tourist offices (Piazza Principe, tel. 010 246 2633 or Via Roma,11 tel.010 576 791). The current price is €15.

Via Garibaldi

PALATIAL VIA GARIBALDI

Another black-and-white striped structure is the Gothic Palazzo Spinola dei Marmi, which was built in the 15th century – and the Spinola, the Doria, the Grimaldi, the Lomellino, the Lercari and the Pallavicino all bring us to Genoa's largest and most magnificent avenue, the **Via Garibaldi**, once referred to by the much-travelled Madame de Staël as the *Rue des Rois*, or 'street of kings'.

The New Street of the 16th century nobility, Via Garibaldi is one of the most fascinating histori-cal urban areas in Europe. Valuable buildings, still intact today, look out onto the street – some of

Map on pages 20–21

👁 Via Garibaldi

Before Via Garibaldi was laid out between 1558 and 1583 with 11 palazzi, there was a great deal of property speculation, forced confiscations and purchases. After three public auctions, the city sold land along a 250m (820ft) stretch of road to five wealthy families, who hired architects to build an elite district, high on the slope and away from the narrow, dark streets of the Old Town. For once, the Doria family were not among them: Andrea Doria, who ruled Genoa during the mid-16th century, had settled down in the magnificent Palazzo del Principe in the west of the city instead.

them are owned by the City Council, like Palazzo Rosso and Palazzo Bianco, which house the most important art galleries in the city from the modern era, with period rooms and furnishings. To coincide with Genoa's accolade as European Capital of Culture in 2004, this street of palaces has undergone massive restoration. Once again, the baroque facades are revealed in all their glory, and the Bianco and Rosso palazzi glow anew.

The Pallavicino family commissioned the Cambiaso (No 1) and Carrega Cataldi (No 4) palaces, the Lomellino family the Palazzo del Podestà (No 7) and the Palazzo Campanella (No 12), the Lercari family the Palazzo Lercari-Parodi (No 3), the Spinola family the Palazzo Gambaro (No 2), Palazzo Spinola (No 5), Palazzo Doria (No 6) and the Palazzo Cattaneo-Adorno (Nos 8–10), and the Grimaldi family had an earlier version of the Palazzo Biano (No 11) built here, along with the **Palazzo Doria Tursi**, which today is the Town Hall (open Mon–Fri 8am–12.30pm & 2.30–5pm: tel 010-557 2223). Nicolò Paganini's violin is kept here in the Sala della Giunta (Council Room) and a funerary urn reported to contain the ashes of Christopher Columbus. Behind the severe facades of these palazzi there are elegant inner courtyards and magnificently decorated rooms, containing many works of art – see for yourself in the Palazzo Rosso or the Palazzo Bianco.

Palazzo Doria Tursi

GALLERIE

Between 1671 and 1677, the Brignole Sale family had the Palazzo Rosso built on the Via Garibaldi, and today its magnificent halls contain the **★★Galleria di Palazzo Rosso ⑩** (open Tues–Fri 9am–7pm, Sat and Sun 10am–7pm, closed Mon), testifying to the taste and culture of this noble family. The collection is stunning, with highlights including works by Veronese, Titian, Tintoretto, Caravaggio, Salvatore Rosa, Guercino and Guido Reni, Van Dyck, Dürer, Ribera and Murillo.

During the early 18th century, the Brignole also converted a Grimaldi palace into the Palazzo Bianco, filling it with sumptuous decoration in the rococo style; today the building houses the newly restored **Galleria di Palazzo Bianco** ⓫. Alongside the most famous names in Ligurian art, such as Ludovico Brea, Luca Cambiaso, Bernardo Strozzi and Alessandro Magnasco, there are several Dutch masters including Gérard David, Hugo van der Goes, Jan Provost, Peter Paul Rubens and Antony Van Dyck, and the two Spanish painters Zurbaran and Murillo are also represented. This is one of the city's finest art collections.

Anyone in urgent need of a break after all this art can take the *ascensore* (lift) from the Galeria Garibaldi to the Spianata di Casteletto, with its Belvedere Montaldo; the panoramic view across the roofs and towers and the harbour is well worth the detour.

MAJESTIC CHURCH

From the Via Garibaldi, cross the Largo della Zecca to reach the early 17th-century church of **Santissima Annunziata del Vastato** ⓬ (open Mon–Sat 7–11.30am, 4–6.30pm, Sun 7–11.30am, 4.30–6.45pm). The neoclassical portico leads into a very richly decorated yet harmonious interior, full of marble intarsia work, stucco and frescoes, with 17th-century Genoese altar paintings by Luca Cambiaso, Domenico Piola, Bernardo Strozzi and other local artists.

Star Attraction
● Galleria di Palazzo Rosso

Below: Palazzo dell'Università
Bottom: Palazzo Reale

Map on pages 20–21

Hall of Mirrors
Don't miss the magnificent opulence of the Hall of Mirrors (Galleria degli Specchi) in the Galleria di Palazzo Reale. Among the fine furnishings and frescoes, there are also exquisite marble sculptures, including Francesco Schiaffino's marble group, *Rape of Proserpina*.

VIA BALBI

The Balbi family must have paid a small fortune to build seven family palaces along today's **Via Balbi** between 1602 and 1620. The 17th-century **Palazzo dell'Università** ⓭ was originally a Jesuit college, and its elegant inner courtyard with its loggias and porticoes is worth a visit. Another place always open for public view is the **Palazzo Reale** ⓮ on the other side of the street; it was named after the kings of Savoy and originally built as a residence for Stefano Balbi between 1643 and 1655. Architect Carlo Fontana extended the building during the 18th century, converting it into a magnificent palazzo, and today it greets visitors in the traditional Genoese colours of red, yellow and green. The baroque and rococo rooms on the first floor house the ★★ **Galleria di Palazzo Reale** (open Tues and Wed 9am–1.30pm, Thur–Sun 9am–7pm), with a frescoed hall of mirrors and a fine collection of paintings and sculpture, including works by Van Dyck and Tintoretto and frescoes from the 17th to 19th centuries.

Statue in the Galleria di Palazzo Reale

VIA DI PRÉ

The park, with its imaginative paving mosaics, contrasts pleasantly with the harbour and the **Via di Pré**, situated below the palace. The busy, cosmopolitan atmosphere of the Via di Pré is very different from the magnificence of the Palazzo Reale. Everything's for sale here, from T-shirts and electronic appliances to smuggled cigarettes and sex. Nevertheless, this place is more of a restaurant district than a red-light one. With all the *trattorie* and *friggitorie*, everything seems very Neapolitan, and the various altars and niches containing madonnas and saints contrast with the irreverent activities going on just beneath them.

MEDIEVAL HOSPICE

Genoa is a harbour city, and Crusaders and pilgrims heading for Jerusalem used to depart from here regularly around 800 or 900 years ago. Thousands of these medieval pilgrims and warriors used to stay in the 11th-century hospice, known as the **Commenda di Pré**, while they were waiting for ships bound for the Orient. The complex of medieval buildings has been admirably restored, and contains the church of San Giovanni di Pré (1180).

In contrast, the ★★**Palazzo Doria Pamphilj**, also known as 'Palazzo del Principe' (open Tues–Sun 10am–5pm, closed Aug, tel: 010-255 509), has lost much of its former splendour. Andrea Doria started building this palazzo when he first came to power in 1528, and five years later it provided accommodation for his patron, Emperor Charles V. Around the middle of the 16th century, the magnificent palazzo extended from the sea (with a private Doria harbour) to the hillside. Its halls, filled with frescoes by Perin del Vaga, a student of Raphael, and its hanging gardens, terraces, fountains and statues formed a model for later Genoese Renaissance structures. This 'paradise', as the palazzo and its grounds were once named, now suffers from the busy, traffic-choked streets and the railway line. However, its recent restoration gives an insight into its former grandeur, and it is not to be missed.

EXCURSIONS

The Genoese always felt threatened from the landward side, and they erected the first defensive

Star Attractions
● **Galleria di Palazzo Reale**
● **Palazzo Doria Pamphilj**

Below: street market
Bottom: Genoa's waterfront

Map on pages 20–21

Best possible view
Those wishing to end this tour with a pleasant impression of the city should make for the the Piazza Principe and board the rack railway to Granarolo. The view, 220m (720ft) above the Old Town, of the harbour and the Lanterna lighthouse, is most impressive, especially towards evening.

wall as long ago as AD200. Over the centuries it was extended to adapt to the city's changing needs, and between 1626 and 1632, when Genoa feared an attack by the ever-mightier House of Savoy, the seventh city wall was built: a 12,650-m (41,500-ft) long 'Great Wall' extending across the hilltops around the harbour city, much of which still survives to this day.

Even this wasn't enough for the Savoyards, who ruled Genoa from 1815 onwards: they gave the wall at least a dozen forts, and today these are the principal sights of the Parco Urbano delle Mura, opened in 1990 and covering an area of 876 hectares (2,165 acres).

RIGHI

Those eager to do the tour of these forts, either on foot or by mountain bike, should take the 1.5km (1mile) rack (funicular) railway (the valley station is on the Largo Zecca) up to the 302-m (1,000-ft) high ★ **Righi**, one of the best observation points in the city.

Pass the red-brick, 19th-century Torre della Specola to reach the Forte Castellaccio. This fort, restored during the 19th century, was a scene of Guelph-Ghibelline strife in medieval times, and though it is well situated, it is not always open to the public. The Osteria di Richettu, right next to the fort, is a good place to stop for rest and refreshment.

Wayside Madonna

FORTE SPERONE

Further north on the Monte Peralto, at the highest point of the city wall, is the mighty **Forte Sperone**. With towers, embrasures, casemates, powder magazine, and various halls and storage rooms, this is a real citadel; it's open to visitors and is often the scene of cultural events, especially open-air summer theatre performances. There's a commanding view from the Forte di Sperone westwards across the forts of Begato and Tenaglia, and the forts of Richelieu, Ratti and Quezzi to the east.

FORTE DIAMANTE

There are more military structures to visit. From Forte Sperone, climb up to Forte Puin, past the atmospherically situated Forte Fratello Minore to **Forte Diamante**. This fort dates from 1756 and is situated at 667m (2,190ft), making it the highest of all the fortresses and the apex of Genoese military engineering, erected after Austrian troops occupied this strategic ridge above the city wall.

On a clear day the view from the star-shaped terrace is spectacular, extending along the Western Riviera to Ventimiglia, with the Ligurian Alps in the distance. Nearby there are some original 'ice-holes': 5-m (18-ft) deep pits into which snow was placed during the winter to provide the city with ice for several months.

Just east of Genoa is the picturesque fishing village Boccadasse. Pastel-coloured houses cluster around the harbour, making this a very photogenic spot, where time appears to stand still.

Villa Doria-Centurione, an early 16th-century structure in the suburb of **Pegli**, houses the restored ★ **Museo Navale** (open Tues–Fri 9am–1pm, Sat 10am–1pm). The exhibition shows the harbour's development and growth of the sailing ship and motor vessel construction industries. The reconstructed caravels in which Columbus sailed to America are fascinating, as are the navigational charts dating from various centuries.

Below: Genoan resident
Bottom: messing around
on the water

Map
on pages
20–21

Wall tour
No other Italian city possesses a long defensive wall in such good condition, and even if military architecture fails to interest you, this tour (4 to 5 hours on foot, 3 hours by mountain bike) has several breathtaking views. In addition, botanists have found more than 900 different species of flora growing wild up here, from the deciduous forests on the northern slopes to aromatic Mediterranean *macchia* on the southern ones.

SUBURBAN VILLAS

Before the villa suburb of Pegli was turned into a centre of tourism in the middle of the last century, Michael Canzio built the ★ **Villa Durazzo Pallavicini**, and, since he was a theatre impresario, he also laid out a magnificent ★ **park** all around it, with splendid views (open Apr–Sept: 9am–7pm; Oct–Mar: 10am–5pm; closed Mon). This highly romantic location has now been successfully restored, and the park contains a tropical garden filled with palm trees, a forest of camellias, and various grottoes and fountains. The villa itself houses the **Museo Civico di Archeologia Ligure** (open Tues–Fri 9am–7pm, Sat & Sun 10am–7pm), which alongside its extensive archaeological exhibits also has a good ethnological collection.

The eastern suburb of Albaro, best reached on a 15 or a 41 bus, is dominated by the ★ **Villa Giustiniani-Cambiaso**. The architect Galeazzo Alessi (1512–72) was influenced by Roman models when he built this Renaissance structure, and it became a basis for many more Genoese villas. Begun in 1548, the building is distinctive for its ground- and first-floor loggias and its scenic location. Today, it houses Genoa University's engineering faculty, but the grounds are open to the public.

★ **Nervi**, a villa suburb east of Genoa, is famous for the panoramic sea promenade, known as the **Passeggiata Anita Garibaldi**, and for its well-tended parks (especially the rose garden in the Parco Grimaldi) and artistic villas, many now museums. The **Villa Serra** contains the Galleria d'Arte Moderna (open Tues–Sun 10am–7pm), with a comprehensive collection of Ligurian painting from the 19th and 20th centuries; the **Villa Grimaldi** has the Modern Art Gallery, the 'Raccolta Frugone', with a superb collection of 19th- and 20th-century Ligurian paintings (open Tues–Fri 9am–7pm, Sat & Sun 10am–7pm, closed Mon); the **Villa Luxoro** (open Tues–Fri 9am–1pm, Sat 10am–1pm, closed Sun and Mon) houses the **Museo Civico Giannettino Luxoro**, with its fine examples of Genoese furniture and paintings dating from the 17th and 18th centuries.

Nervi

2: VIP Territory

Recco – Camogli – Portofino – Santa Margherita Ligure – Rapallo – Chiavari – Lavagna (Valle Fontanabuona) – Sestri Levante (approx 50km/30 miles)

Map on page 40

This route takes us along the Riviera di Levante, or Eastern Riviera, where one wealthy community follows hard on the heels of the next. Camogli's narrow little fishermen's houses are among the most-photographed sights in Liguria. Portofino is very exclusive indeed, and Santa Margherita and Rapallo contain artistic villas set amid romantic parks. Zoagli's weavers used to supply princes and cardinals with velvet and brocade. Sestri Levante is very romantically situated in its half-moon shaped bay, and hosts the Hans Christian Andersen fairytale prize annually. Allow yourself one day to cover this route.

Below: relaxing in Camogli
Bottom: Camogli harbour

RECCO

The trip begins in **Recco** to the east of Genoa and follows the Via Aurelia, successor to the ancient Roman road and as much travelled now as it was in antiquity. Recco is a bell-making centre. Ever since the early 19th century, when a few families who had emigrated to Germany returned to their native Liguria, church clocks

Map below

were manufactured here and bells cast – also in the neighbouring villages of Avegno and Uscio higher up the mountain. Today the resort is bereft of character, after World War II bombardments destroyed its substance; it has never managed to keep up with the more famous towns nearby. Gastronomically, however, Recco comes into its own as one of the bastions of Ligurian cuisine. The pancake-like *focaccia* (locally called *fugassa al formaggio*), filled with cheese then oven baked, is generally regarded as the very best in Liguria.

Steep steps, Camogli

CAMOGLI

A lot of people come to **Camogli** just to eat. On the second Sunday in May, several hundredweight of fish are fried in 500 litres of oil, inside a frying pan 4m (14ft) in diameter – and there's free fish for everyone. That's not the only reason to visit, however: with tall, narrow and colourful *case-torre* fishermen's houses, it is one of the most photographed towns on the coast. 'Camogli' derives from *casa mogli* or 'house of wives', as the women would run the port while their menfolk were at sea. The reason the facades are so colourful is so that homecoming fishermen could recognise their houses from afar; today there are cafés, restaurants

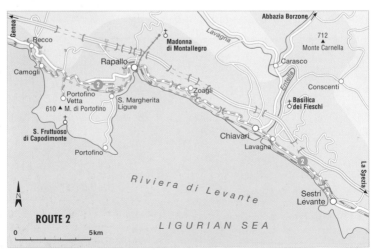

Abbazia Borzone
Genoa
Recco
Lavagna
712
Monte Carnella
Madonna di Montallegro
Rapallo
Carasco
Camogli
Zoagli
Conscenti
Portofino Vetta
S. Margherita Ligure
Basilica dei Fieschi
610 ▲ M. di Portofino
S. Fruttuoso di Capodimonte
Chiavari
Portofino
Lavagna
La Spezia
Riviera di Levante
N
ROUTE 2
Sestri Levante
LIGURIAN SEA
0   5km

and a sunshade-covered beach along the coast here. The maritime museum, **Museo Marinaro 'Gio Bono Ferrari'** (open Oct–Mar: Mon 9am–noon, Thur and Fri 9am–noon, 3–6pm; June–Sept: Wed, Sat, Sun and holidays 9–noon, 4–7pm), documents the golden age of sea travel during the 19th century, when Camogli had a larger fleet than Genoa and would rent it out to warring nations. Around 3,000 sailing ships were built here during that time.

High on a rocky outcrop, the Basilica di Santa Maria Assunta is visible from afar, with its neo-classical facade, and the forbidding-looking single tower of the 12th-century Castel Dragone beside it. Inside, the ultra-modern **Acquario Tirrenico** (open summer: daily 10am–noon and 3–7pm) shows the kind of fish that swim in the Golfo Paradiso off Camogli – every angler's dream!

SAN FRUTTUOSO DI CAPODIMONTE

The ★★ **Benedictine Abbey of San Fruttuoso di Capodimonte** (open Mar–May: 10am–4pm; June–Oct: 10am 6pm; closed Nov–Feb except holidays) can be reached by a 30 minute boat trip from Camogli, past the Punta Chiappa, but it is also an excellent three-hour hike. There are several magnificent views across the coast and the resorts, and the heady aroma of wild strawberries, gorse, rock roses, rosemary and myrtle make this tour unforgettable. The hike can also be continued: Portofino is just two hours further away. When the sea is too choppy and the ships are forced to remain at anchor in the harbour, San Fruttuoso is only accessible by foot.

The abbey's history stretches far back into the Middle Ages. When the Arabs attacked Spain in the early 8th century, Bishop Prosperus of Tarragona left his country and came to Italy to seek refuge. The sunny hills around Portofino and the Mediterranean vegetation may have reminded him of his lost homeland. To create a suitable home for the relics of St Fructuosus, which the bishop had brought with him, a church and a monastery were soon built. It wasn't safe from attack, however, and was destroyed in the 10th

Watery memorial
San Fruttuoso is famous for the Cristo degli Abissi (Submerged Christ). Symbolic of the contrast between Camogli's sea-faring wealth and the loss of life at sea, this bronze statue of Christ by Guido Galletti was submerged 17m (56ft) below the surface in 1954. On the last Sunday in July, wreaths are laid at the feet of the statue in a ceremony to commemorate those who have perished at sea.

The ferry to San Fruttuoso

Map on page 40

Below: Portofino café life
Bottom: hotels by the harbour

century before being rebuilt by Benedictines. In the 13th century, it was renovated by the Doria family and the abbot's palace was added. Six members of the Doria family were buried here between 1275 and 1305. In the crypt, the Gothic tombs with the vertical 'Doria strip' made of white marble and black stone are very impressive. San Fruttuoso is anything but remote these days: people lie soaking up the sun only a few yards away. The abbey is no longer as special as it once was, but its location in a (formerly) remote bay, and the buildings overgrown with vegetation, make an excursion here memorable nevertheless.

Monte di Portofino

San Rocco, above Camogli, is a starting-point for hiking trips up ★★ **Monte di Portofino**, the highest mountain in the Monte di Portofino Nature Reserve. At 610m (2,000ft) Monte di Portofino is no Mount Everest, but the all-round view from the top is still impressive, and on clear days you can see as far as Elba and Corsica. Botanists have documented more than 700 plant species up here.

Portofino

To get to ★★★ **Portofino** take the narrow coast road, which on summer weekends is hopelessly jammed from Santa Margherita onwards. This has advantages, however: it gives you longer to admire the villas along the way with their magnificent parks, the rocky cliffs and romantic bays.

The Phoenicians were among the first to realise that the bay of Portofino was the safest natural harbour along the Ligurian coast: it is sheltered from the wind and accessible whatever the weather. The Romans, whose ships set sail for Gaul from here, called the town *Portus Delphini*, the 'dolphin port'. When tourism arrived, Portofino soon became a haunt of the rich and famous. Instead of star-spotting down at the yacht harbour, however, take a walk through olive groves to the lighthouse out on the **Punta del Capo**; you will pass the magnificently situated 12th-century church of San Giorgio (restored in 1950) and also the **Castello Brown** (open daily 10am–7pm), a Genoese bastion built to defend the Gulf. Its origins date from medieval times, and it was redesigned in the 16th–18th centuries to become the private residence of Yeats Brown, the British consul in Genoa, in 1870.

Car-free Portofino is the most fashionable and exclusive resort on the Italian Riviera. 'Carefree with your wallet' must be the advice if you plan to find accommodation here, but the famous luxury Hotel Splendido is worth a look as one of the world's most beautiful hotels.

Much photographed, filmed and frequented by the rich, famous, yachties and the merely curious, this utterly enchanting harbour town was first discovered by the British in the 19th century. Often imitated, as in Sir Clough Williams Ellis's fantasy village of Portmeirion in North Wales, Portofino's spectacular location is like a film set, and still draws visitors in their thousands, including film directors and their stars.

SANTA MARGHERITA LIGURE

A less exclusive and reserved town than Portofino is **Santa Margherita Ligure**, also located at the foot of the Monte di Portofino. The people are young and keen on entertainment, and the hotels cater to all tastes. The palm-lined beach promenade

Star Attraction
● Portofino

Diving centre
Boat trips with underwater viewing equipment are popular, and there is scuba diving all year. For information on diving, contact the Diving Centre of Santa Margherita Ligure: tel: 0185-293017.

Below: Portofino skipper
Bottom: the marina

is just the place for a relaxed stroll and an espresso, and beyond the Riviera park (open daily 9am–7pm, 5pm in winter), with all its exotic plants and statues, is the elegant Renaissance **Villa Durazzo**. These days this impressive building, which dates from 1560, provides an atmospheric backdrop for chamber music concerts. The new Museo V.G. Rossi, devoted to the author Vittorio Rossi, is now open in the Villa Durazzo (open daily 9.30am–6.30pm, 4.30pm in winter).

Before Santa Margherita Ligure was discovered by the jet set, it was – like all the other Riviera resorts – a small fishing community. Because of this it's a good idea to visit the church of **Sant'Erasmo**, the patron saint of sailors, and get a feel of local history. The paintings inside show the kinds of dangers to which local fishermen and mariners were often subjected out in the Mediterranean. The small town netted so much fish that it became a desirable place to conquer, however, and Lombards, Saracens and Venetians were all in charge here at different periods in history. In the 16th century the town was taken by the notorious pirate Dragut; today it's been invaded by tourists. The locals have kept tourism successfully in check in some respects, however: the olive groves and oak forests around the town have yet to make way for the anonymous residential complexes that are often such an eyesore elsewhere.

Below: Santa Margherita harbour
Bottom: Rapallo promenade

RAPALLO

These days the only reminder of ★ **Rapallo**'s dangerous past, when the locals had to fend off pirate attacks, is the small 16th-century **fort** at the harbour. Today this busy town, the third 'pearl' along the Golfo del Tigullio after Santa Margherita and Portofino, is a major tourist centre.

The palm-lined beach promenade, the Lungomare Vittorio Veneto, features old-fashioned art-nouveau buildings and charming cafés with glass verandas; small music groups still perform in the early 20th-century Chiosco della Banda Cittadina. Those interested in liturgical implements will find a collection of processional crosses next door to the church of Santo Stefano in the **Oratorio dei Bianchi** (daily 10am– noon and 3–6pm).

Rapallo, too, lived almost exclusively from fishing until the mid-19th century, when the first tourists came to enjoy its mild winters. While the men were away at sea, the women whiled away the time by lacemaking. The finest of these bobbin lace products can be admired in the ★★**Museo del Merletto** (open Tues, Wed, Fri and Sat 3–6pm, Thur 10 11.30am, Sun by request, tel: 0185-63305) in the Villa Tigullio. The museum has a display of lace from the 16th to the 20th centuries, including exquisite examples of pillow lace.

One of the biggest festival days in Rapallo celebrates the **Holy Virgin of Montallegro** at the start of July. The whole town makes its way up to the church of Nostra Signora di Montallegro, 612m (2,000ft) up in the mountains. The church can also be reached by car or by cable car (cable car open Mar–Oct Mon–Fri 9am–12.30pm, Sat and Sun 8.30am–12.30pm). Its rather lurid neo-Gothic facade takes some getting used to.

ROAD TO CHIAVARI

The resorts of **Lorsica** and **Zoagli**, on the way to Chiavari, have specialised in clothmaking for centuries, and their products were much sought after by kings and heads of state. The firm of Gaggioli still uses an 18th-century loom to weave its satins. The cloth here is very expensive – it takes one day to produce just 3m (10ft) of it.

Star Attraction
● Museo del Merletto, Rapallo

The Irish view
The writer W.B. Yeats liked to escape the Dublin winter and visit his friend Ezra Pound in Rapallo. He described the town in *A Packet for Ezra Pound*, written in 1929: 'Houses mirrored in an almost motionless sea, mountains that shelter the bay from all but the south wind, bare brown branches of low vines and of tall trees blurring their outline as though with a soft mist: a verandahed gable a couple of miles away bringing to mind some Chinese painting, and Rapallo's thin line of broken mother of pearl along the water's edge.'

Lacework in the Museo del Merletto

Map
on page
40

Below: Piazza Mazzini and (bottom) the Palazzo di Giustizia, Chiavari

Along the road to Chiavari there are several fine views of the coastline between Portofino and Sestri Levante. Soon the late 14th-century pilgrimage church of ★**Madonna delle Grazie** comes into view, perched high above the sea at 177m (580ft) . The interior contains an important fresco cycle by the Ligurian artist Teramo Piaggio, depicting *Scenes from the Life of Christ*; the pink and green pastel tones are most attractive.

CHIAVARI

After it has entered the small town of **Chiavari**, the *Via Aurelia* turns into the Via Martiri della Liberazione; the locals simply call it *carrugio dritto* ('straight street'). It is still the main shopping street, just as it was when Chiavari was built as a fortress town by the Genoese in the 12th century to provide protection against the Fieschi on the other side of the Entella river. The ancient necropolis at the foot of the castle hill proves that the area was settled before the Romans came, in the 8th and 7th centuries BC.

The town experienced its golden age during medieval times when it was an important trading post; it was so well protected by its fortress and walls that travellers in the 16th century considered it to be one of the finest walled towns in Europe. The old walls were razed in the 18th

century to make way for new palazzi, including a fine **Palazzo di Giustizia** in Piazza Mazzini.

Today, Chiavari is a modern seaside resort. The most impressive structures are the mighty baroque **cathedral**, rebuilt in the 19th century, the medieval **Palazzo dei Portici Neri** and the broad **Palazzo Rocca** (1629) and its park (open daily 7am–7pm). Palazzo Rocca also contains the Museo Archeologico per Preistoria e Protostoria (open Tues–Sat 9am–1.30pm, and 2nd and 4th Sundays in the month), documenting finds from the pre-Roman necropolis and the Tigullio Gulf.

LAVAGNA

The bridge across the Entella is all that separates Chiavari from neighbouring **Lavagna**, which has a huge yachting marina. While the inhabitants of Chiavari were loyal subjects of Genoa, the counts of Fieschi in Lavagna enjoyed centuries of proud independence. In the 13th century, Pope Hadrian V, a member of this powerful noble family, had a ★★ **Basilica dei Fieschi** (open daily 8am–noon, 1.30–6pm, till 7pm in summer) built in the nearby village of San Salvatore dei Fieschi. The grey-slate and white-marble striped façade, the Gothic portal with its lunette fresco, the rose window and the unpretentious interior make it one of the most attractive Romanesque-Gothic structures in Liguria. Along with the Palazzo Comitale next door, it is a fitting symbol of the power once wielded by the Fieschis.

SESTRI LEVANTE

Sestri Levante is a lively seaside resort, but the old centre retains a traditional Ligurian atmosphere. The long promenade, which extends the length of the Baia delle Favole ('Bay of Fables'), is just as romantic. At the highest point of the long promontory, the Isola, is the 12th-century church of San Nicolò dell'Isola, and nearby is the Parco dei Castelli, with the **Marconi Tower**, where Guglielmo Marconi (1874–1937) first experimented with high-frequency radio.

Star Attraction
● Basilica dei Fieschi, Lavagna

Evocative names
Hans Christian Andersen gave the pretty northern bay the name Baia delle Favole, 'Bay of Fables' during his stay in 1833. Perhaps even more beautiful is the Baia del Silenzio, 'Bay of Silence' on the southern side, adorned with lovely pastel-coloured houses. Of all the photogenic views on the Italian Riviera, Sestri Levante is blessed with two of the most stunning.

Basilica dei Fieschi, Lavagna

Map
below

Below: Riomaggiore
Bottom: Vernazza locals

3: The Cinque Terre

Levanto – Monterosso al Mare – Vernazza – Corniglia – Manarola – Riomaggiore (approx 45km/27 miles)

The five villages that make up the ★★★ **Cinque Terre** ('Five Lands'), with their colourful houses bunched closely together, cling to the rocky coast like eagles' nests. Lord Byron described this stretch of coast as 'paradise on earth'. Until the last century the locals drank their own wine, cultivated with difficulty up on the steep slopes, and the area was very remote.

Today, the Cinque Terre's tiny villages of steep, narrow streets and miniature squares have become a UNESCO World Heritage Site, and the area has been designated a National Park. But because access to them by car is virtually impossible, it has been spared mass tourism. This makes conditions even more ideal for the many hikers who come here for the well-marked routes, breathtaking views and comfortable restaurants.

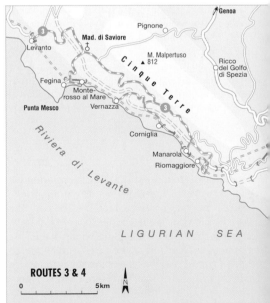

WALKING ROUTES

Although it is theoretically possible to visit the Cinque Terre by car, the tiny roads leading to the villages of Monterosso, Vernazza, Corniglia, Manarola and Riomaggiore are narrow, steep and full of bends, and the few car parks have already been claimed by the locals. The Cinque Terre can only be properly appreciated on foot, and for keen walkers they are one of the best regions in Italy. You can walk from one village to the next and travel back by train to your starting-point, or take the ancient 9 mile (14km) 'Blue Way' (★**Sentiero Azzurro**) high above the sea, through the different villages.

In springtime, however, the route tends to be crowded. Possible escape routes in this event would be the Sentiero Rosso No 1, which goes up as high as 700m (2,300ft) but requires the right equipment, or the easier Strada dei Santuari, which runs along the slope and connects five pilgrimage churches. Each of the five villages has one of these churches situated above it.

Star Attraction
● **Cinque Terre villages**

The villages are also linked by ferry

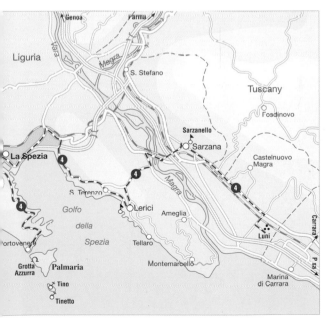

Map on pages 48–49

Local Laureate

The Ligurian poet Eugenio Montale (1896–1981), who won the Nobel Prize for Literature in 1975, spent many childhood and early adulthood summers at the family villa in Monterosso. Always fascinated by the waves and rough seashores, he contrasts the constantly changing force of the sea with human frailty and limitations in his 1924 poem *Mediterraneo*, which begins:
Ancient one, I am drunk with the voice that escapes from your mouths when they lift open
like green bells and thrust back again, backwards and fall away.

LEVANTO

It's a good idea to start your tour of the Cinque Terre in **Levanto**. Although just outside the Cinque Terre and the province's fourth largest town, this is a pleasant and elegant resort with quite a few good sights. The Loggia del Comune on the Piazza del Popolo, with its arcades and Romanesque capitals, dates from the 13th century, and the Gothic parish church of Sant'Andrea with a Ligurian striped facade is 30 years older. A bas-relief on the Oratorio di San Giacomo (16th-century) reminds us that the ancient pilgrimage route to Santiago de Compostela passed through Levanto.

MONTEROSSO AL MARE

The walk from Levanto to Riomaggiore, the farthest of the five villages, takes around four hours. It's best to travel by train as far as **Monterosso al Mare**, the Cinque Terres's most westerly village. The special atmosphere – houses huddled together, steep alleys, and fishing boats pulled up as far as the village piazza – is rather absent here, but Monterosso still has the only stretch of coast in the vicinity that could be called a beach. The pilgrimage church, built between the 13th and 14th centuries, is the oldest in all the villages. **San Giovanni Battista** is Gothic, and its consecration to John the Baptist is a reminder that this stretch

Corniglia

of coast was held by Genoa from 1276 onwards. The artists who came here were also Genoese: the works of 16th- and 17th-century Luca Cambiaso, Bernardo Castello and Bernardo Strozzi can be admired in the Capuchin church of San Francesco (1619) on the slope. The **Sentiero Azzurro** (No 2, with the blue-and-white markings) to Riomaggiore follows the medieval routes used for transporting goods. Tiny gardens full of greenery, ancient olive groves and carefully-tended vineyards line the route, which provides views across breathtaking stretches of coastline. The soil on the terraces was brought here with great difficulty, and can be washed downhill again by heavy rain.

VERNAZZA

The most attractive of the Cinque Terre, ★ **Vernazza**, comes into view. It is the only one of the five villages that has a natural harbour. Its buildings seem to form part of one single labyrinthine structure; narrow streets lead past portals with reliefs, dominated by a medieval round tower that, like the rectangular Saracen tower by the harbour, has outlived its usefulness. The locals congregate in the small piazza behind the 14th-century parish church of **Santa Margherita d'Antiochia**, right beside the harbour; its octagonal bell-tower is a distinctive feature of the village.

CORNIGLIA

Unlike the other villages, **Corniglia** does not lie next to the sea but extends along a 100-m (330-ft) outcrop like the prow of a ship. This village, the smallest of the five, is famed for its full-bodied white wine, *Sciacchetrà*, which is difficult to find in the shops. No less delicious is the *Cinque Terre* DOC white wine, also made from Albarola, Bosco and Vermentino grapes. The parish church of **San Pietro**, built in 1334 above the remains of an 11th-century chapel, has a fine Carrara marble rose window and a Gothic portal. The view from the Belvedere terrace is almost dizzying; there are 377 steps down to the coast.

Perfect beach
The village of Corniglia is perched over the Cinque Terre's best and most beautiful beach. Lying on the northern side of the promontory, this perfect beach, the Spiaggia di Guvano, is lapped by clear, warm water, just one of the few in Liguria where nudity is permitted.

Below and bottom: around Vernazza

Map on pages 48–49

The High Road
The Alta Via delle Cinque Terre first leads to the scenic Punta Mesco near Monterosso, then to the 330-m (1,000-ft) high Colla di Gritta and the pilgrimage church of Madonna di Saviore (which also provides food and lodging). From here follow route number one, which reaches its highest elevation at the Sella di Malpertuso (780m/2,500ft) and provides a good impression of Liguria's 'two faces': the blue sea on one side, and the green, lonely mountains on the other.

The path to Manarola

MANAROLA

At the railway station at the foot of the steps, the walk continues to ★ **Manarola.** The pink, brown, yellow and light-green houses that so attracted Swiss artist Paul Klee huddle together, as if fearful of losing their balance and toppling over the steep rock face into the sea. Many say this is the most spectacularly picturesque of the five villages. There's a 14th-century Gothic parish church here, too: **San Lorenzo**, with its marble rose window. The piazza in Manarola is so small and the harbour so tiny that the colourful fishing boats have to be pulled up on to the land.

RIOMAGGIORE

The last section of this route takes us to **Riomaggiore**. The **Via dell'Amore** connects Manarola with the last of the five villages via a comfortable flight of steps hewn out of the rock face. This route was laid out in the 1920s – not for romantic walks in the moonlight but for quick access to a nearby powder magazine. However, the 'Path of Love' is scenically beautiful and a relatively easy mile-long walk. Even though the village can be reached by road from La Spezia, the whole place is still redolent of times past. One of the first tourists to come to Riomaggiore was the painter Telemaco Signorini, the leading representative of the Italian 'Macchiaioli' art movement, devoted to Impressionist painting in natural surroundings. The main street of Riomaggiore from the station to the church is named after him. Riomaggiore is also the HQ of the Cinque Terre National Park set up in 1999. The Gothic church of **San Giovanni Battista** was the last of the Cinque Terre churches to be built, and dates from around 1340.

For the experienced, there is a good hike from Levanto to Riomaggiore along the **Alta Via delle Cinque Terre**, which follows the ridge between the Vara Valley and the Ligurian Sea *(see box)*. The whole mountain tour takes eight or nine hours, and the right equipment is essential. Along the path there are red and white wild strawberry flowers, and yellow gorse.

4: Harbours Past and Present

Portovenere – La Spezia – Lerici – Montemarcello – Sarzana – Luni (approx 85km/52 miles)

Map
on pages
48–49

La Spezia has been one of the chief naval ports of Italy for the past 150 years, and its naval arsenal has given it a military feel; several battles took place here in past centuries too, most of them centred round the medieval castle of Lerici. Today, however, La Spezia and the region around it are far less well-known for past deeds of valour than for astonishingly beautiful landscape. Several famous Romantics lived here, including Lord Byron, Percy Bysshe Shelley, and the Swiss painter Arnold Böcklin. Shelley later lost his life in a boating accident off Livorno.

Below and bottom: around Portovenere

Portovenere, formerly a pirates' lair, is a delightful Italian village. Sarzana, a popular meeting-place for antiques dealers from all over Italy, is dominated by a Medici fortress. International trade flourished in Luni around 2,000 years ago; today, only atmospheric ruins remain of the Romans' greatest marble harbour. This route needs a whole day.

PORTOVENERE

Experienced seafarers as they were, the medieval Genoese knew a safe harbour when they saw one. When they purchased ★★ **Portovenere** in 1113,

Map
on pages
48–49

they gave this small fishing village enough forti-fications to withstand even the worst pirate attack. As a Genoese border post, Portovenere had to be prepared for enemy attack at any time; it was most likely to come from either pirates or from the Pisan castle in Lerici just across the Gulf. This is why the houses in Portovenere form a wall along the shore, and also why the streets are so narrow: they could be closed off within seconds and bolted shut. If conditions got really dangerous, the cliffs could be smeared with tallow to make them slippery, and the women would pour boiling oil or tar over the heads of the enemy. Simple – but effective.

Below: Portovenere castle
Bottom: San Pietro church

SIGHTS IN PORTOVENERE

Genoa knew just how strategically important Portovenere was, and treated it with great respect over the centuries. The **castle**, built in 1162 and extended in the 16th and 17th centuries, domi-nates the town. The Romanesque church of **San Lorenzo** was built even earlier, and was con-secrated in 1830 by Pope Innocent II; later it received Gothic and Renaissance additions. There is a fine *Martyrdom of St Lawrence* in the lunette on the main portal. A nocturnal procession to the church takes place on 17 August every year, and the building looks most impressive by torchlight. The annual procession on 29 June to the church

of **San Pietro** is no less impressive. The church is splendidly situated on a rocky cape, and dates from 1250. Its four-arched loggia was added later, and affords a magnificent view of the Cinque Terre as far as Punta Mesco and across to the marble mountains of Carrara. Beneath it, at the foot of the hill, the Grotta Byron commemorates the great English Romantic poet, who would often come here after a long swim to declaim his verse.

A long flight of steps leads back to the colourful bustle of the Calata Doria at the harbour. Narrow alleys lead from here to the Via Capellini, the pretty main street, where several elegant slate and marble house portals can still be seen.

ISLANDS TO VISIT

One real must for anyone visiting Portovenere is the 10-minute boat trip out to the ★ **Isola Palmaria**, a rocky island full of caves and covered with *macchia*, where the ruins of several Stone Age dwellings have been discovered. The remains of the 11th-century Abbey of San Venerio are on the far smaller **Isola del Tino**, which may be visited only for the Festival of St Venerio on 13 September and the following Sunday.

LA SPEZIA

When Napoleon conquered Liguria in 1797, he was particularly delighted by **La Spezia**, which at that time was a fishing community with around 3,000 inhabitants: 'It is the finest harbour in the world, better fortified even than Toulon, and can be defended just as easily from the land as from the sea.' France's emperor had ambitious plans for the town: he wanted to turn it into a military harbour and increase its population by 12,000. More important considerations and the vagaries of politics left him no time to implement this, however, and the idea was only taken up again in 1860 by the new Kingdom of Italy. La Spezia was given an arsenal and then a trading harbour. Today, the town is the second-largest in Liguria (pop. 91,279) and, after Genoa, the most important

Star Attraction
● Portovenere

The White Madonna
There is a legend that a small painting of the White Madonna in San Lorenzo's marble altarpiece was brought to the church from the sea in 1204. On the night of August 17 1399, it apparently the subject of a miracle when it was transformed into its present state. The miracle is commemorated annually in a hugely atmospheric torchlit procession on August 17.

Piazza Verdi, La Spezia

Map
on pages
48–49

naval base in Italy. Ferries sail from here to Corsica during the summer, but from a tourist's point of view, La Spezia isn't all that inviting; the place is modern and largely anonymous.

GREAT MUSEUMS

Some sights are definitely worth seeing, however. Beside the arsenal is the **★★Museo Tecnico Navale** (open Mon–Sat 8.30am–6pm, Sun 10.15am–3.45pm; July and Aug: 8.30am–1.15pm, 4.15–9.45pm), with fascinating models of Roman and Greek triremes and galleys, caravels of the type used by Christopher Columbus on his voyages to the New World, Bourbon sailing ships and 20th-century Italian motor vessels. The collection of ships' figureheads is just as fascinating: the bare-breasted Atlanta, discovered in 1864, must have turned quite a few heads on board.

Below: figureheads and (bottom) exterior, Museo Tecnico Navale

The city's latest museum is the award-winning **★★ Museo Amadeo Lia**, opened in 1997 (open Tues–Sun 10am–6pm). Patron of the arts Amadeo Lia collected the works that now embellish 13 rooms in the beautifully restored 17th-century Paolotti convent in Via del Prione. The 13th- and 14th-century paintings are among Europe's most important private collections. Other masterpieces include works by Titian, Tiepolo, Pietro Lorenzetti and Giovanni Bellini.

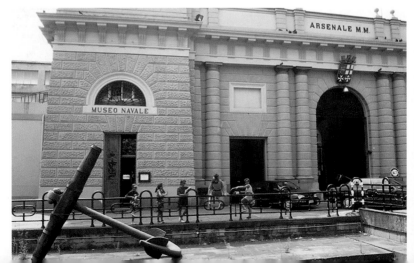

There are miniatures, medals, precious bronzes and archeological finds – a real treasure trove.

CASTLE AND CATHEDRAL

The mighty **Castello San Giorgio** was built in the 13th century by the powerful Fieschi family, and later extended by the Genoese. Recently restored, it houses the **Museo Archeologico 'Museo Civico Ubaldo Formentini'** (open summer 9.30am–12.30pm, 5–8pm, closed Tues; winter 9.30am–12.30pm, 2–5pm, closed Tues), which documents the distant past. It includes the Bronze Age ★★**stelae** that were discovered in the nearby Lunigiana, and stone statues of figures found on the bed of the River Magra.

At the foot of the hill is the church of **Santa Maria Assunta**. The magnificent *Coronation of the Virgin* terracotta inside, by Andrea della Robbia (1500), makes up a bit for the fact that the building had to surrender its cathedral status to the church of ★ **Cristo Re**. This new cathedral, with a circular ground-plan, was designed by Adalberto Libera (1903–63), a leading proponent of the Rationalist movement in the 1920s and 30s. La Spezia has a number of examples of modern art. The Quartiere Umberto I, north of the Museo Civico, was laid out as a working men's residential community during the 19th century, in imitation of the French *cités ouvrières* and the Krupp community in Essen.

GULF OF POETS

The broad bay off La Spezia is also known as the 'Gulf of Poets'; the villages on its east side, with their picturesque houses and pretty landscape, attracted a number of the romantically inclined during the 19th century. Swiss painter Arnold Böcklin and the two English poets Byron and Shelley all stayed in **San Terenzo**. In June 1822 Shelley began working on *The Triumph of Life* here, and it was in July that he drowned in a boating accident after visiting Byron and Leigh Hunt. His body was washed ashore on 18 July,

Below: Bronze Age stelae
Bottom: Cristo Re

Map on pages 48–49

and Byron cremated it on a funeral pyre at Viareggio. The Casa Magni, from which Shelley embarked on his last journey, sailing to Livorno, contains a small museum devoted to his life and work, but its future is now uncertain since the house was recently sold.

LERICI

Below: Lerici
Bottom: Tellaro

The construction boom from tourism has turned San Terenzo and **Lerici** into one large community, and robbed both towns of much of their individual charm. Lerici is dominated by its imposing medieval **castle**, which was built by the Pisans in 1241 as a counterbalance to the Genoese fortifications in Portovenere. The Pisans' good fortune didn't last long, however: the castle was firmly in their Genoese rivals' hands by 1256. An inscription on the entrance portal to the Gothic castle chapel of Sant'Anastasia glorifies this victory.

The Geo-Palaeontological Museum inside the castle is also worth a visit. Dedicated to the prehistory of the Gulf, the age of dinosaurs is brought to life by robotics and simulated figures. There is also a room with an earthquake simulator. (Open Tues–Sun 10.30am– 12.30pm, 2.30– 6pm; July and Aug: 10.30am–12.30pm, 6.30pm– midnight; winter: 10.30am–12.30pm, 2.30–5.30 pm.)

TELLARO

There are several tiny bays and atmospheric caverns and grottoes along the coast between Lerici and **Tellaro**, a traditional Ligurian fishing village with an impressive church and colourful houses. D.H. Lawrence lived from 1913 to 1914 in nearby Fiascherino, which at that time was very remote.

MONTEMARCELLO

Situated on a rocky point, ★★**Montemarcello** faces the bay like a ship's figurehead. Narrow streets between grey and pink houses, the smell of jasmine and a magnificent view have attracted many Milan VIPs and intellectuals, and several old mills, farmhouses and medieval watchtowers have now been converted into desirable residences.

Medieval Montemarcello was a bastion against the Saracens, and in World War II the Germans used it to supervise the nearby 'Gothic Line'.

Star Attraction
● Montemarcello

AMEGLIA

Ameglia can either be reached either along a mountain road, or via the coastal resort of **Bocca di Magra**, which for years was the home of the writer Elio Vittorini. Tall, narrow farmhouses and fishermen's cottages dating from the past three centuries are clustered round the castle hill, and from the square in front of the church there is a superb view of the Plain of Luni and the marble-white Apuan Alps in Tuscany. In 963, during the reign of Emperor Otto I, it was mentioned as the official seat of the bishops of Luni. On a gustatory note, Ameglia's restaurants enjoy a high reputation.

Roman footsteps
The beautifully located hill-top village of Montemarcello takes its name from the Roman consul Marcellus, who vanquished Liguria. The surrounding Montemarcello-Magra Regional Nature Park is rich in Mediterranean fauna and flora, and from here it's possible to walk down to the sea on the well-marked footpaths. The strategic importance of the foothills was well-known to the Romans, who defended their marble quarry at Luni.

SARZANA

The town of **Sarzana** was built from the 11th century by people escaping the nearby marshland of Luni. In 1204, Luni had to surrender its bishopric to Sarzana, and from that moment on the town achieved unparalleled popularity with Pisa,

Montemarcello

Map on pages 48–49

Napoleon's home
The main road through Sarzana is the Via Bertoloni, which joins the Via Mazzini running to the southeast. Once part of the Via Francigena, the early pilgrims' route to Rome, today's road includes the town's main squares and, of particular note, the house and tower at No.28 which belonged to Napoleon Bonaparte's family, before they emigrated to Corsica.

Sarzana antique market

Lucca, Genoa, Milan and Florence for its favourable military and commercial location. The mighty **citadel** was built on the orders of Lorenzo the Magnificent in 1488, and the architects involved in its construction included the great Renaissance fortress builder Giuliano da Sangallo. The Fortezza di Sarzanello, on a mound to the northwest of the town, is even more impressive. Built on a triangular ground-plan, it retains its forbidding appearance despite much restoration and its current use for cultural purposes.

The old part of town is also distinctive for its Tuscan architecture. The Romanesque-Gothic ★ **cathedral of Santa Maria Assunta** (13th–15th-century) with the monument to Sarzana's most famous son, Pope Nicholas V, contains a collection of fine works of art that includes the ★ *Cross of Master Guglielmo* (1138) and two 15th-century winged altarpieces by Leonardo Riccomanni from Pietrasanta in Tuscany.

STREET MARKET

Today Sarzana (pop. 20,000) is a sophisticated town with excellent shops, where in past centuries conditions were very different. During medieval times, pilgrims passed through along the *Via Francigena* to Rome and the Holy Land. Now, pedlars come to Sarzana every August from all over Italy to sell at the street market (*Soffita in Strada,* 'Attic on the Street'), while the town's antiques dealers exhibit in the Palazzo degli Studi.

LUNI

★★ **Luni** lies less than a mile from the Tuscan-Ligurian border. The Romans laid it out as a fortress in their fight against the Ligurians during the 2nd century BC, and it soon developed into a busy harbour. The merchandise traded here included wine and cheese, wood from the dense Apennine forests, and above all marble from the Apuan Alps – all shipped directly to Rome. Carrara and its marble quarries are just a stone's throw away, and the pure, snow-white marble from the

Apuan Alps – or *Lunae Montes* as they were then known – was very much in demand in Rome.

After Rome fell, demand for marble from Luni slackened off. Over the centuries, the Magra river washed so much alluvial material down to its delta that the town began to silt up. Malaria broke out in the surrounding marshlands, and most of the population moved to Sarzana, leaving their once-glorious marble harbour behind. Excavations of the **Roman site** in 1837 revealed a forum, theatre, amphitheatre, a temple of Diana and several magnificent villas with frescoes and mosaic floors, such as the 3rd-century Casa dei Mosaici and the Casa degli Affreschi. This is the most important archaeological site in northern Italy.

ARCHAEOLOGICAL MUSEUM

Luni's **Museo Archeologico Nazionale** (open Tues–Sun 9am–7pm), with finds from recent excavations, is well located in the centre of the ancient town. Statues and busts of emperors testify to the high artistic level of the ancient harbour of Luni, which today lies 2km (1 mile) from the sea. The museum provides fascinating insights into marble quarrying and working during Roman times. The amphitheatre in the ruined city once held 5,000 spectators; it is now an atmospheric venue for summer theatre and ballet performances.

Star Attraction
● **Luni**

Below: sculpture at the Archaeological Museum and (bottom) Roman ruins, Luni

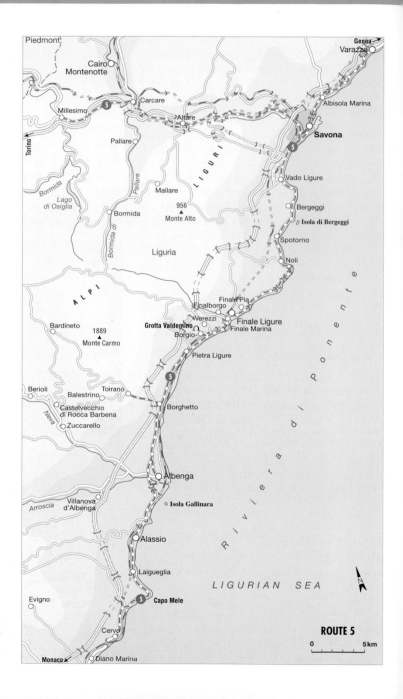

ROUTE 5

0   5km

5: Art, Ceramics and Chamber Music

Varazze – Albissola Marina – Savona – Noli – the Finales – Borgio-Verezzi – Toirano – Albenga – Alassio – Laigueglia – Cervo – Diano Marina (100km/62 miles not including excursion inland)

Map on page 62

Star Attraction
● Monte Beigua Nature Reserve

Today's ceramic artists in Albissola are so prolific that the entire beach promenade is paved with their work. Noli and also the many-towered town of Albenga were enriched by medieval artists; the fine piazza in Verezzi is transformed into an open-air theatre in the summer; and the square outside the church in Cervo is used for international chamber music performances. Culture plays an important role in the towns and villages along this route, which also leads back into the dim prehistoric past inside the Caves of Toirano. The provincial capital of Savona is modern, and from its harbour Fiats and Lancias are exported around the world . Allow two days for this trip – three if you feel like exploring the mountains inland.

Below: Sant'Ambrogio and (bottom) the port, Varazze

VARAZZE

The town of **Varazze** possesses a yachtbuilding centre and marina and a mile long sandy beach. The parish church of **Sant'Ambrogio** is built above the foundations of a Romanesque-Gothic structure from which the campanile survives. The church contains a polyptych of *St Ambrose with Divine and Music-Making Angels* by the Genoese artist Giovanni Barbagelata (1500) and a *Virgin* by the 16th-century Ligurian, Luca Cambiaso.

NATURE RESERVE

The main attraction of Varazze, however, is the nearby **★★Monte Beigua Nature Reserve**, only a 20-km (12-mile) drive away. Monte Beigua itself is 1,287m (4,220ft) high, and the trip is worthwhile for the magnificent panoramic view from the top alone, which on a clear day extends north to Monte Rosa and south as far as Corsica. This mountain massif is only 6km (4 miles) or so from the sea as the crow flies, and the contrast between south-facing Mediterranean vegetation and north-facing mountain flora is nowhere more apparent. The bare, serpentine rock walls have provided many Ligurian architects with construction material over the centuries, and several unique ★**cave drawings** have also been discovered, thought to be 5,000–6,000 years old.

Below: promenade and (bottom) beach, Albissola Marina

ALBISSOLA MARINA

Work of more modern artists is a feature of **Albissola Marina**, reached via the resort of Celle Ligure. Albissola is in two parts: Albissola Marina is on the coast; Albisola Superiore slightly inland. The different spelling reinforces their separate identities, though both are famous for their ceramics of local clay, decorated in blue and white. The series of coloured tiles along the Lungomare degli Artisti beach promenade parallel to *Via Aurelia* is by contemporary Italian artists such as Giuseppe Capogrossi, Roberto Crippa, Agenore Fabbri, Lucio Fontana and Aligi Sassu, and also the Dane Asger Jorn and Cuban Wifredo Lam.

Albissola's ceramic artists follow an unbroken tradition dating from the 16th century. The history of the industry features in the **Museo del Centro Ligure per la Storia della Ceramica** (open Mar–Sept: Tues–Sun 3–7pm) in the Villa

Faraggiana. Ceramics are the main focal point in Albisola Superiore's **Museo della Ceramica Manlio Trucco** (open June–Sept: Tues–Sat 6pm–10.30pm, Sun & Wed 10am–12.30pm; Oct–May: Tues–Fri 3.30–7pm, Sat 10am–7pm, Wed & Sun 10am–12.30pm). Also in Albisola Superiore, the Villa Gavotti gives a fascinating glimpse of the lives of the 18th century nobility.

SWEET SASSELLO

A good detour for gourmets is the tourist town of ★ **Sassello**, famous for small almond-flavoured *Amaretti* biscuits and its flower festival, the *Infiorata (see page 109)*. It's 23 km (14 miles) away and 405m (1,330ft) up in the mountains. The route leads past the rather inconspicuous-looking village of **Stella**, where the politician Sandro Pertini (1896–1990) was born and buried. Persecuted and imprisoned under the Italian Fascist regime, he was president of Italy from 1978 to 1985.

An excellent town

Sassello was the first Ligurian town to be awarded an 'Orange Flag', the coveted symbol of excellence conceived by the Touring Club of Italy and the Regional Authorities to promote tourism in inland Liguria. As well as being very pretty, it is also the headquarters of the Visitors' Centre for the Monte Beguia Regional Nature Park, the home of interestingly varied flora and fauna, including prized wild boar.

SAVONA

★ **Savona**, an important harbour town for more than 2,000 years, is today as important as ever as the export harbour for Fiat and Lancia cars. Historically, Liguria's third largest town (pop. 61,997) has been inextricably linked with the nearby smaller community of Vado Ligure. Whenever one experienced an economic upswing, the other suffered. During the Punic Wars, Savona backed Hannibal, but Vado enjoyed Roman support; the early Middle Ages saw Savona in the ascendent, then Vado until the 10th century when King Berengar II made Savona the capital of part of the Ivrea Marches, giving Vado a subsidiary role. In the early 16th century, Savona's harbour was filled in by the Genoese, fearing competition, and in World War II the town suffered aerial bombardment.

Below: arcaded street and (bottom) harbour, Savona

CONTEMPORARY HIGHLIGHTS

To see some interesting contemporary architecture, go to the western part of town and take a look at

Map on page 62

the main railway station (1960) and the Palazzo della Provincia (1964), both of them designed by the famous Italian architect Pier Luigi Nervi (1891–1979). Otherwise, a walk through the old town by the harbour suffices to gain a good impression of what Savona has to offer.

MEDIEVAL TOWERS

By the harbour there are still three towers dating from the Middle Ages; one of them, the **Torre de Leon Pancaldo**, is named after the mariner from Savona who accompanied Magellan on his voyage round the world in 1521. In the 15th century the della Rovere family grew very powerful, and Sixtus IV and Julius II (the two family members who became popes) were very generous to their native town. Sixtus IV had a **Sistine Chapel** built on to the cathedral cloister to house his parents' tombs; it received its present-day rococo glory in the 17th century. In 1495 Giuliano della Rovere, later to become Pope Julius II, commissioned the Tuscan architect Giulio da Sangallo to build the Palazzo della Rovere (no public admission). Around a century later the cathedral was built, but the Genoese conquered Savona in 1528 and had the entire area, including the cathedral and the episcopal palace, razed to the ground. In its place they built the mighty Fortezza del Priamar, to dissuade their new subjects from contemplating any thoughts of rebellion.

Below: medieval towers and (bottom) Sistine Chapel, Savona

CATHEDRAL TREASURES

The town's cathedral is in the Piazza del Duomo, north of the Priamar fortress. The adjoining **Museo del Tesoro della Catedrale** is where the cathedral treasure is kept (open on request, donation required), and inside the church are some magnificently carved early 16th-century choir stalls, valuable gold and silver artefacts and also works by the Renaissance painters Ludovico Brea, Luca Cambiaso and Albertino Piazza. The nearby rococo chapel of Nostra Signora di Castello contains a polyptych by Vincenzo Foppa and Ludovico Brea.

GENOESE FORTRESS

To get a proper feel of Savona, take a stroll along the main shopping street, the Via Paleocapa, and down the medieval side-streets – or walk up to the ★ **Fortezza del Priamar**. The present fortress was built by the Genoese in 1542. Inside, the **Museo Archeologico** (open June–Sept: Tues–Sat 10am–noon, 5–7pm, Sun 5–7pm; Oct–May: Tues–Sat 10am– noon, 3–5pm, Sun 3–5pm) has impressive necropolis and archaeological finds from the Iron, Bronze and Roman periods, and several North African mosaic floors from the 3rd and 4th centuries, while the **Museo Sandro Pertini**, on the ground floor of the Palazzo della Loggia in the fortress, has contemporary drawings and sketches. On the third floor is an extensive 16th–20th-century ceramic collection in the ★ **Pinacoteca Civica**, which was re-opened in July 2003 after extension and renovation (open Mon–Sat 8.30am–1pm, 6.30pm on Thur).

ALTARE

Glass production in **Altare**, a village 15km (9 miles) outside Savona, may be older than the famous Murano glass. It was probably introduced in the 11th century by Flemish masters, but never achieved the international reputation of its Venetian competitors. Alongside the larger factories

Mazzini's cell
Priamar Fortress takes its name from *pietra sul mare*, 'stone above the sea', and is a majestic garrison and a superb example of 16th-century military architecture. The fortress has been central to the town's history: Romans, Byzantines and Lombards all fortified it, and the people of Savona successfully defended themselves against attacks by Saracens, French and Milanese. Once used as a prison to the revolutionary *Risorgimento* (Italian unity) fighter, Giuseppe Mazzini in 1830–31, it is now an important museum complex.

Savona from Fortezza del Priamar

Map
on page
62

there are still several small establishments where glass is hand blown. The **Museo del Vetro** (open Tues 3–6pm; Thur 9.30am–12.30pm and Sat 10am–noon and 3–5pm) has several exhibits of local glassware, including a bottle 130cm (51 inches) high, thought to be the world's largest.

Below: Altare glassware
Centre: Millesimo
Bottom: Noli seafront

MILLESIMO AND BACK

Travel via Ferrania now for another 15km (9 miles) as far as the village of **Millesimo**. Like many communities inland, it is dominated by its castle, the del Carretto castle; its arcaded main square, on which stands the originally Romanesque church of Santa Maria extra Muros (15th-century fresco fragments), is a romantic place for a rendezvous.

The best way of getting back to the coast at this point is to drive along the Turin-Savona motorway, which is very scenic all the way to **Vado Ligure**. This harbour for crude oil products also contains a **Museo Civico** (open Mon, Thur and Sat 9.45am–12.45pm; Tues, Wed, Thur and Fri 3–6.30pm) with Roman and medieval finds, as well as works by the sculptor Arturo Martini (1889–1947).

NOLI

The route continues via Bergeggi, with an island of the same name (now a nature reserve, closed

to the public and populated by seagulls), and past the built-up resort of Spotorno, with a medieval castle, to arrive in ★★**Noli**. This little resort was once a focal point of international politics. Noli grew rich and influential during the First Crusade in 1097 and became an independent maritime republic shortly afterwards. During the years that followed, Noli – the smallest maritime republic in Italy – fought alongside Genoa against Venice and Pisa, and it was only in 1797 that it finally lost its independence, to Napoleon.

The Loggia della Repubblica, with original cobblestones, commemorates Noli's glorious past, as does the 'Regata Storica dei Rioni' which takes place on the second Sunday in September.

Gastronomic Noli
Surrounded by olive groves, Noli is a good place to linger in a beautiful setting over Ligurian specialities. Try delicious pastries at Pasticceria Scolvini, Via Colombo, 3. Or the excellent local wines and traditional Ligurian gastronomy of the restaurant Lilliput, at Voze, Via Zuglieno, 49, tel: 019-748 009 9 (3km/2 miles from Noli).

CASTLE AND TOWERS

Noli has retained its flair more successfully than the other resorts along the Riviera. The 12th-century ruined **castle**, with fortifications stretching from the castle hill to the town walls, is just as impressively scenic as the ancient streets, with their buttressed houses and the five brown towers. Noli is thought to have had as many as 70 of these towers in the 13th century, when shipowners and captains had the right to build a tower house at least 50m (160ft) high.

A ROMANESQUE CHURCH

The church of ★**San Paragorio** (open summer: Tues, Thur, Sat, Sun 10am–noon; winter Thur 10am–noon) is one of the most important Romanesque structures in Liguria. It was built above the ruins of a previous early Christian building in the mid-11th century. The stone sarcophagus on the north side of the church dates from that time. The facade is decorated with arched friezes in the Lombard style, and its three irregular apses face the sea. Highlights include a Romanesque lectern, a wooden episcopal throne (12th-century), the remains of a 15th-century fresco, and a remarkable 12th-century wooden crucifix that portrays Christ in a tunic.

Noli castle

Map
on page
62

THE CATHEDRAL

The cathedral of **San Pietro** (13th- and 16th-century) is also worth a quick visit; its medieval structure is still very much in evidence, despite several early baroque alterations. Just outside the Gothic gate on the eastern side of town is the large lemon-yellow church of **Nostra Signora delle Grazie**, built in the 18th century, with white rococo decoration on its facade. From the square in front of it there is a fine view of Noli and its bay, especially towards evening. Alongside all the art and history, present-day Noli still hasn't lost its original charm either. It has retained a 'fishing village' atmosphere more successfully than the other Ligurian coastal communities; the fishermen here still pull their nets up on to the beach, and sardines in brine from Noli make a good souvenir.

Below: Varigotti
Bottom: Finalborgo

THE FINALES

Continue along the *Via Aurelia* now, through **Varigotti** with its colourful houses, as far as ★ **Finale Ligure**, which actually consists of three separate communities: Finale Pia, Finale Marina and Finalborgo. **Finale Marina**, an important trading centre in the old days, is now a modern and well-equipped seaside resort with a fine sandy beach and a palm-tree-lined promenade. In the Piazza Vittorio Emanuele II, an imposing-looking triumphal arch commemorates the visit here by the Spanish-Habsburg heiress Margherita in 1666, on her way to Vienna to marry the emperor Leopold I. The baroque church of San Giovanni Battista, built above the ruins of an early Christian basilica dating from the 5th–8th centuries, is surrounded by elegant 16th-, 17th- and 18th-century town houses and palazzi.

FINALE PIA

During medieval times, **Finale Pia** grew up around the church of Santa Maria di Pia; its facade is rococo and its interior baroque, and the only surviving Romanesque-Gothic feature is the 13th-century campanile. The abbey next to it was founded by the Benedictine Order in the 16th century; the monks brought their own ceramic artists with them from Tuscany, and the work here is strongly influenced by the Della Robbia school.

FINALBORGO

The most attractive of the Finales is ★★ **Finalborgo**. Its situation a short way inland has spared it the architectural excesses of tourism, and its 15th-century centre is almost completely intact. The town was founded by the margraves of Carretto after an earlier settlement had been destroyed during their wars with the Genoese. There is no shortage of photogenic spots, and vegetable shops and stand-up cafés are housed inside elegant palazzi with stuccoed ceilings. Past and present make an attractive combination, and there's nothing museum-like about this busy town.

Before you visit one of the restaurants for a *pasta con pesto* (a typical pasta or noodle dish with basil sauce which is an absolute must in Finalborgo, a town renowned for its basil), pay a brief visit to the parish church of **San Biagio**. Its late Gothic campanile, built on top of one of the old fortification towers, is the town's most famous landmark, and the baroque interior contains some fine 18th-century marble sculpture.

*Below: view from
Castel Gavone
Bottom: Finalborgo*

Map on page 62

A 15-minute walk from here leads to **Castel Gavone**, an impressive complex of ruins, and all that survives of a mighty 15th-century fortress. The only remaining major part is the **Torre dei Diamanti**, with diamond-patterned walls. It makes an excellent subject for a photograph, and also contains several interesting fresco fragments.

A real must in Finalborgo is the **Museo Archeologico del Finale** (open summer: Tues–Sun 10am–noon and 3–7pm; till 10pm on Wed and Fri; Oct–May: 9am–noon and 2.30–5pm), housed inside a cloister of the former monastery of Santa Caterina. The collection, documenting the history of the Finales, features Roman, medieval, Stone Age and Ice Age finds from the region.

Below: Castel Gavone
Bottom: church of San Biagio

VAL PONCI

A good way of soaking up the history of this region is to take a short trip eastwards from Finale Pia to the **Val Ponci**. Five Roman bridges dating from the 2nd century (three of them are in remarkably good condition) show how efficient the Romans were at roadbuilding, even in 'provincial' areas. The *Via Julia Augusta* used to pass this way; it was built in AD13, and restored by the emperor Hadrian (who had the bridges added) in the 2nd century. It is possible to hike from here to the Altopiano delle Manie, a limestone plateau with fascinat-

ing flora and fauna. The earliest inhabitants of Liguria used the caves in this region 300,000 years ago. There are primitive drawings on the rockface, known as the Ciappo del Sale, showing figures, crosses and abstract human forms. The Romans used this region later as a quarry.

BORGIO-VEREZZI

There are also several caves in the region around **Borgio-Verezzi**, and the limestone cavern, known as the **Grotta Valdemino** (open May–end Sept: Tues–Sun 9–11.30am and 3–5.30pm; 1 Oct–30 Apr: Tues–Sun guided tours 9.30, 10.30 and 11.30am and 3, 4 and 5pm), with its stalactites, is worth a visit. There are a lot more attractive sights in this double resort (**Borgio** is by the sea; **Verezzi** up on the slope above), however: such as the parish church in Borgio, with its magnificent neoclassical facade, and the church of Santo Stefano's interesting Romanesque-Gothic features.

PIETRA LIGURE

Pietra Ligure and Loano are modern and built-up – something relatively unavoidable for small resorts along the narrow Ligurian coast. Their older sections still have a quaint charm of their own, however. **Pietra Ligure**, one of the Western Riviera's oldest settlements, is dominated by a castle (medieval, with later alterations). The Castello in **Loano** is a magnificent 17th-century palace surrounded by a park, erected by Giovanni Andrea Doria *(see page 14)*. The Doria, who ruled the town almost without interruption from 1477 to 1737, also built the Convento di Monte Carmelo, where tombs in the family mausoleum were erected until 1793. The steep ascent to this attractively situated Carmelite convent is worth it for the views and the landscape alone.

TOIRANO

From the anonymous-looking seaside resort of Borghetto Santo Spirito, a trip to ★★ **Toirano**

Star Attraction
● Toirano

Dramatic setting
Verezzi, standing at 200m (650ft), is in a different world. Its four tiny localities of Poggio, Piazza, Roccaro and Crosa are reminiscent of a medieval Saracen village, with square houses all huddled together around cobbled streets. Piazza, the largest of the four, has a peaceful Piazza Sant'Agostino, where first-class theatre performances are held from mid-July to the beginning of August against a scenic backdrop. The luxuriously-planted slopes, with walled terraces, thick with olive trees, vineyards and almond trees, are a feast for the eye. In the evening, lights from the coastal resorts are spectacular.

Borgio-Verezzi

Map on page 62

(3km/2 miles) is a must. There are several magnificent medieval buildings and palazzi with slate portals, but the nearby limestone caverns are the village's real claim to fame. The **Museo Etnografico della Val Varatella** (open daily 10am–1pm and 3–6pm) contains collections of fossils and primeval implements and ceramics that were discovered in the caves surrounding the town. It's even more fascinating to visit the **Grotte di Toirano** caves themselves, however (open daily 9am–noon and 2–5pm, guided tours). The footsteps of a Cro-Magnon man were discovered in the first cave, the **Grotta della Bàsura**, or 'Witch's Grotto'; he lived there 15,000 years ago and fought giant cave bears on a regular basis. The sparkling minerals in the neighbouring **Grotta di Santa Lucia** make it a truly magical subterranean cavern.

Below: Grotta della Bàsura
Bottom: the baptistry, Albenga

BALESTRINO

The houses in the nearby village of **Balestrino** seem on the point of sliding down the steep slope, and have been deserted by their occupants – a typical example of inland depopulation in Liguria, where steep, eroded slopes make life very difficult if not downright impossible.

ALBENGA

After the narrowness of the Riviera, the sheer expanse of the fertile plain around ★★ **Albenga**, with fruit and vegetable plantations, is a dramatic contrast. The real highlight of Albenga is its medieval architecture: the early Christian baptistry, the Romanesque-Gothic cathedral, high medieval towers and old palazzi combine to produce an absolutely magnificent old town.

The entrance to the ★★ **baptistry** is situated at the foot of a flight of steps, some 2m (7ft) beneath today's street level, which has changed due to the numerous floods that have afflicted the town throughout the centuries. The building is Liguria's earliest Christian building. It has 10 outer walls, but is octagonal inside, and dates back to the 5th century. An unfinished font stands at the centre of the chapel. Twelve doves encircle the monogram of Christ in a priceless Byzantine mosaic dating from around AD500, decorating the principal apse opposite the entrance. The floral ornamentation on the tomb to the right of the entrance is 8th-century Lombard work.

The cathedral of **San Michele** was built at the same time as the baptistry, but its present appearance dates from the 13th century. Three Renaissance lions guard the attractive ★ **Piazza dei Leoni** outside the main apse.

Star Attractions
● Albenga and its baptistry

MUSEUMS

Albenga was originally founded as *Albium Ingaunum*, and conquered by the Romans in 181BC when they were securing a direct route to Spain. The old part of Albenga has inherited the rectangular Roman grid pattern of streets, but the most important traces of its heritage can be found in its museums. The **Civico Museo Ingauno** (open daily except Mon 10am–12.30, 2.30–6pm in winter; 9.30am–noon, 3.30–7.30pm in summer), housed inside the 14th-century Palazzo Vecchio del Comune, contains remains from the ruins of the Roman city of Albenga. The **Museo Navale Romano** (opening times as Civico Museo) also has some fascinating finds. Its collection includes

Below: Museo Navale Romano, Albenga

Map on page 62

Nightlife
Night life in Alassio centres around its main street, the Via XX Settembre, where cafés and restaurants stay open until the early morning hours, and on the promenade, Passeggiata Italia, where discos throb until very late.

Below and bottom: Alassio

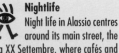

around 10,000 wine amphorae that were part of the freight of a Roman ship that sank off Albenga in the 1st century BC. In 1925 a fisherman found several of the amphorae in his net, but it was only in 1950 that the cargo, 40m (130ft) down, could finally be brought ashore; the ship itself is still down there to this day.

The **Pontelungo**, a many-arched bridge built across the Centa by the Romans as part of *Via Aurelia*, was left to decay when the river changed course but has nevertheless survived the centuries.

ALASSIO

The town of **Alassio** has now completely surrendered to tourism. Rather than promoting its ancient monuments and works of art like Albenga, Alassio promotes its mild climate, its long sandy beach and its entertainment centres. The church of **Sant'Ambrogio**, with its fine Renaissance slate portal, is almost obscured from view by the colourful bustle in the town centre. Its magnificent baroque interior contains several paintings by Genoese artists of the 16th and 17th centuries. Alassio's main attraction is the **Muretto** ('little wall'), covered with colourful ceramic tiles with autographs of such luminaries as Ernest Hemingway, Louis Armstrong, Dario Fo, Giuseppe Guareschi and Sandro Mazzola.

The **Isola Gallinara** lies off the coast of Alassio and Albenga. Its wealth of flora and fauna has made it a regional nature reserve, and because of this it is closed to the public, but you can take a boat trip from Alassio around the island.

LAIGUEGLIA

The far more peaceful town of **Laigueglia** is now almost a part of Alassio, but unlike its noisier neighbour, it still retains the atmosphere and appearance of a Ligurian fishing village. The majolica tile decoration on the dome of the 18th-century baroque parish church of **San Matteo** is playfully naive. It's possible to drive 3km (2 miles) from Laigueglia to nearby **Colla Micheri**, but walking is a better idea. In 1958 Thor Heyerdahl, the famous Norwegian explorer and archaeologist, fell in love with this tiny hillside village, bought it and restored it.

CERVO

Cervo is a picture book Ligurian village, high above the sea. Every summer a chamber music festival is held in the scenic square outside the baroque church of **San Giovanni Battista**.

Narrow streets lead up from the church to the medieval Castello, which contains the ★**Musco Etnografico del Ponente Ligure** (open daily; summer: 9am–12.30pm, 3–7pm and July–Aug 4.30 10pm; winter: 9am–12.30pm, 3–6pm), a fascinating museum documenting rural and maritime life in the Cervo region.

DIANO MARINA

Just 2km (1 mile) from Cervo lies **San Bartolomeo al Mare**, a popular tourist village where the medieval church, **Madonna della Rovere**, tends to get overlooked for the beach activities. Also popular with visitors is **Diano Marina**, 3km (2 miles) down the road; the village is best known for its flower festival, the *Infiorata (see page 109)*, when the streets are covered in petals.

Below: Laigueglia beach
Bottom: Cervo church steps

Map on pages 80–81

6: Olives, Oil and Spaghetti

Imperia – Pieve di Teco – Molini di Triora – Triora – Taggia – Arma di Taggia – Bussana-Vecchia (100km/62 miles)

This is definitely a route for gourmets. It begins at the Olive Museum in Oneglia and leads through glorious countryside to Pieve di Teco, formerly a popular rest-stop for medieval salt transporters. Triora is notorious for its witch trials, held in 1587, while tourists flock to Molini di Triora in September for its 'Snail Festival'.

Art fans will also enjoy this route: the parish church and the Dominican monastery in Taggia are decorated with several valuable old masters. Further along the route, the ruined village of Bussana Vecchia has become a colony for modern artists, sculptors and potters.

Motorists should note that the narrow, winding roads inland require patience and skill, especially between Pieve di Teco and Triora. Because of this it's best to plan at least two days for the trip.

Below: Olive Oil Museum and (bottom) marina, Imperia Porto

IMPERIA

The Impero river once separated the two halves of **Imperia**: the medieval Porto Maurizio, up on a hill on the west side of the Impero delta, and the more modern (and prosperous) Oneglia to the

east. The two communities were joined in 1923 after centuries of rivalry: Porto Maurizio had always been loyal to Genoa, while Oneglia was a harbour for the House of Savoy. To avoid ruffled feelings, the town hall and post office are situated exactly halfway between the two ex-towns.

PORTO MAURIZIO

The inhabitants of **Porto Maurizio** were relying on a long period of economic prosperity when they began building the mighty cathedral of San Maurizio in the late 18th century, but the turmoil of the Napoleonic era soon dashed their hopes. Porto Maurizio never expanded any further than the hills its huddled houses still occupy, and the neoclassical **cathedral** looks incongruously large and pompous. Construction work ended in 1838, rather than in 1781 as originally planned, after the oversized cupola had collapsed and been replaced by a smaller one. The interior contains several paintings by Gregorio de Ferrari and Domenico Piola, two respected Ligurian artists of the early 18th century who paved the way from baroque heaviness to the light and playful rococo style.

Below: the cathedral and (bottom) Via XX Setembre, Imperia-Porto

NAVAL MUSEUM

The ★ **Museo Navale Internazionale del Ponente Ligure** (open Wed and Sat 3–7pm; July and Aug: also 9–11pm), housed together with the Pinacoteca Civica inside a neoclassical building on the cathedral square, documents the history of seafaring on the Western Riviera. There are more than 130 models of sailing ships ancient and modern here, together with a collection of moving votive pictures.

Narrow streets right next to the cathedral lead into the ★ **Parasio** (probably derived from the Roman *palatium*), the old section of town. The originally medieval church of San Pietro, which contains some fine frescoes, rests on the remains of the old town wall. There's a good view across the Riviera from the church parapet, and the loggia-lined promenade of the 18th-century

Convento di Santa Chiara – also built on the ruined town wall – is just a short walk away. Elegant slate portals and sculpture on the palazzi and townhouses remain here alongside the facelift given to the Parasio at the end of the 20th century. This is once more an elegant district.

If you want to experience some real Ligurian atmosphere, have a look at the **Borgo Foce** quarter down by the water below the Paraiso. Here you

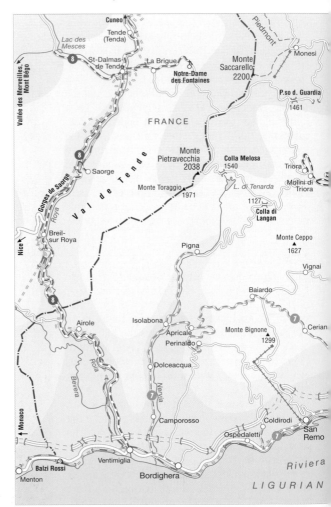

can watch fishermen as they repair their nets or stroll around the nearby **Borgo Marina,** which was built around a medieval hospice belonging to the Knights of Malta.

There's a good detour (10km/6 miles) from Porto Maurizio to the pilgrimage church of ★**Madonna delle Grazie**, built above the spot where, according to the legend, a dumb shepherd girl suddenly began to speak after a vision of the

Borgo Marina
This pretty little fishing village is huddled around the 13th–14th-century church of San Giovanni Battista. A stone tablet recalls the visit of the poet Petrarch in 1343 en route to Avignon, two years after he was crowned as Poet Laureate.

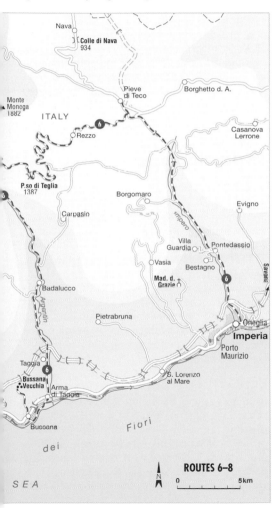

Imperia-Porto marina

Map on pages 80–81

6,000-year-old olive
The Museo dell' Olivo (Olive Tree Museum) in Imperia, Via Garessio 11/13 (open Mon–Sat 9am–12.30pm, 3–6.30pm), is a major Italian private museum, which opened in 1992 and won European Museum of the Year in 1993. It celebrates the olive tree, symbol of the Mediterranean, which, for 6,000 years, has played a leading role in economic, technical, artistic and religious history. Its role in human life is demonstrated by rare and remarkable finds from every period and country, by descriptions and passages from the Bible, Homer, and many other poets and writers.

The olive oil produced in the western Ligurian Riviera is among the most valued in Europe. A staple ingredient of the healthy 'Mediterranean diet', it makes a good souvenir.

Olive groves around Imperia

Virgin. Construction work began on this idyllically situated church in 1450, and its frescoes were painted by the brothers Tomaso and Matteo Biazaci in 1483. The realistic depiction of hell and its torments must have had a salutary effect on sinners over the centuries.

ONEGLIA

The other half of Imperia, **Oneglia**, may not be as historically important as Porto Maurizio, but it does pride itself on having been the home town of Andrea Doria (1466–1569, *see page 14*), the capricious soldier of fortune and politician who gave Genoa 30 years of freedom and independence. The birthplace of this controversial hero lies in the Via – you guessed it – Andrea Doria.

OLIVE TREE MUSEUM

Just behind the railway station in Oneglia, the famous olive-oil manufacturing firm of Fratellie Carli has set up a state-of-the-art ★ **Museo dell'Olivo** (open Mon–Sat 9am–12.30pm and 3–6.30pm) in an art nouveau villa. The 12 departments inside document the history of the ancient art of olive cultivation, which grew so important in the Mediterranean region during medieval times that, even today, 95 percent of olive oil production still takes place there. Botanical and medicinal information, various oil mills and oil presses, and the reconstructed cargo hold of an Ancient Roman freighter are just some of the themes and sights of this fascinating museum.

VILLAGES

Continuing along the valley of the River Impero in the Ligurian hinterland, it is well worth taking time to explore some of the villages that lie off the main road. There are **Bestagno** and **Villa Guardia** above Pontedassio, both of which date back to the Middle Ages, and **Borgomaro**, which was once an important centre for the marketing and distribution of olive oil.

PIEVE DI TECO

Proof that the remote towns and villages further inland were once of far greater importance is amply provided by ★ **Pieve di Teco**. The neo-classical parish church of **San Giovanni Battista** was built between 1792 and 1806 by the Lombard master architect Gaetano Cantone, who also designed the cathedral in Porto Maurizio and the parish church in Pietra Ligure. This region earned the money to pay for its art from its strategic situation on the much-travelled salt routes, which ran from the sea across the Ligurian Alps and Apennine passes to the plain of Piedmont and Lombardy, and intersected in Pieve di Teco.

Below: north of Pieve di Teco
Bottom: Pieve di Teco café

The town was founded in 1233 and contained paper mills, silk factories, ropemaking workshops and weaving centres, and the caravans that transported precious salt from the Ligurian coast across the mountains were very happy to take a break in the shade of the trees along the **Corso Ponzoni**. Elegant palazzi and artistically decorated slate portals testify to the town's former importance. There are plenty of craftsmen's workshops still here today; some of them make the hand-crafted walking boots which are highly prized.

Keen hikers should take a detour from Pieve di Teco to the mountain village of **Monesi** (1,310m/4,300ft above sea level), and scale the highest mountain in Liguria, **Monte Saccarello**

Map on pages 80–81

(2,200m/ 7,200ft). It takes three hours to get to the summit from Monesi. The northern slopes of the mountain are covered with Alpine roses every summer, and its strategic location between Italy and France endowed it with a comprehensive network of footpaths between the two World Wars – making things easy for hikers and climbers.

Below: Molini di Triora
Bottom: Triora doorstep

MOLINI DI TRIORA

A winding road leads from Pieve di Teco via the mountain village of Rezzo to Molini di Triora and Triora. **Molini di Triora** is named after the 23 watermills *(mulini)* in operation here in the late Middle Ages. This sleepy little town comes alive in September during the *Sagra della Lumaca* (Snail Festival). It's an ideal base for excursions and hiking trips; motorists can travel to the broad plain up on the Colle di Langan (1,127m/3,700ft), or to the Colle Melosa (1,540m/5,052ft), where the Franco Allavena refuge hut is located (the key is available from the Club Alpino Italiano, or CAI, in Bordighera). For potholing enthusiasts there are numerous limestone caverns in the Pietra Vecchia Toraggio massif, and mountain climbers can test their mettle on the ★ **Sentiero degli Alpini**, a path hewn out of vertical limestone walls by Italian soldiers between 1936 and 1938. The plan here was to build a secret supply route just in case war broke out between Italy and France – which of course it did soon afterwards. This walk, which should also include a hike around the Monte Pietravecchia (2,038m/6,686ft), is extremely scenic and takes about six hours to do.

TRIORA

Witches, superstition and the black arts are all inextricably linked with **Triora**. In 1587, when a famine broke out in the region, a scapegoat was sought – and found in the shape of 200 women, all of whom were accused of witchcraft and tried in Genoa. Many were tortured, some pretended they met the devil every night to save their lives, and around 15 were condemned to death. The **Museo Etnografico e della Stregoneria** (open Mon–Fri 3–6.30pm, Sat and Sun 10.30am–noon, 3–6.30pm) documents the unfortunate episode in its local history exhibition.

Triora is a pretty village. Cobbled alleyways lead through a labyrinth of picturesque houses, many of which now stand empty because the inhabitants have moved to the big city. Today, Triora has a population of just 300; 40 years ago it was four times that number, and during the late Middle Ages, when there was an important connecting route between the sea, Brigue and Tende, 500 families lived here. The village contains the ruins of five fortresses and castles, three of the original seven town gates and almost a dozen churches and chapels.

The Romanesque-Gothic **Santa Maria Assunta** contains a painting by Luca Cambiaso, and also an altar panel of *The Baptism of Christ* by Taddeo di Bartolo from 1397 – thought to be the oldest painting in Western Liguria.

TAGGIA

Travel via the seaside resort of Arma di Taggia now to reach the culturally important town of ★★ **Taggia**. According to legend, Benedictine monks from Piedmont converted the local population during the 7th century – not only to

Star Attraction
● Taggia

Adrenalin sports
As well as being perfect hiking and climbing country, with sheer rock faces, the area around Triora is also famous for bungee jumping. The Loreto bridge runs 120 metres (395ft) over the Argentina river gorge from where, in summer, a bungee jump is literally breathtaking.

Basketmakers, Triora

Map
on pages
80–81

Dance of Death
In the middle of July, usually the third weekend, the important *Festa della Maddalena* is celebrated in Taggia. The highlight is the late-medieval Dance of Death – a rare performance and unique to this part of Italy nowadays.

Christianity but also to olive cultivation. Olives, citrus fruits, almonds and figs all took the place of the town's traditional dairy farming and maritime pursuits, and soon brought prosperity. Today the churches, magnificent town houses and noble portals all testify to the town's former greatness.

The most attractive of these palazzi can be seen in the Via Curlo, the Via Gastaldi, the **Via San Dalmazzo** and the arcaded Via Soleri, in which an antiques market is held every month. Biblical symbols and the coats-of-arms of noble families can be seen in the reliefs on the slate portals; the Napoleonic revolutionary troops vented their anger on the nobility here in 1797. The medieval bridge across the Argentina river has 16 arches and is 260m (850ft) long; the river becomes a torrent after heavy rainfall. In the upper part of town, the church of **Madonna del Canneto** has a 12th-century crypt, as well as several fine 16th-century frescoes by Giovanni and Luca Cambiaso and also Francesco Brea.

Below: old doorway and (bottom) San Domenico portal, Taggia

DOMINICAN MONASTERY

Francesco Brea's more famous uncle, Ludovico, has many works inside the ★★ **Dominican monastery** (open Mon–Sat 9am–noon and 3–6pm), just outside Taggia's town gates. The Dominicans had arrived here in Taggia in 1468, and between 1483 and 1513, Brea, who was born in Nice in 1450 and died in Genoa in 1523, produced his altar paintings *St Catherine of Siena*, the *Baptism of Christ* and the *Annunciation*, all of them set against Gothic gold backgrounds. During a visit to Lombardy, Brea came in contact with the new Renaissance style, and its influence is clear in his *Madonna of the Rosary*, where the gold background has been replaced by a realistic landscape reminiscent of Leonardo. The earlier Piedmontese artist Giovanni Canavesio, active on the Western Riviera and in the Nice region between 1472 and 1500, did the altar painting of *St Dominic*, also owned by the church. More works by Canavesio and the Breas can be admired in the chapter house and also in the monastery's small museum (open Mon–Fri 9am–noon, 3–6pm), open to visitors on request.

Star Attraction
● **Dominican monastery, Taggia**

BUSSANA-VECCHIA

From old-fashioned art to modern art now: a road leads from Arma di Taggia up to the village of ★ **Bussana-Vecchia**, where a colony of artists and craftsmen have lived since the 1960s. This magnificently situated village was destroyed by an earthquake in 1887, and while the new town of Bussana was being built at a different site down by the sea, the mountain village of Bussana-Vecchia fell into decay. The houses and walls collapsed and became overgrown. The only survivor of the earthquake was the landmark campanile of Sacro Cuore.

During the 1950s, several families from the south of Italy who had come to Liguria to work in the flower industry tried briefly to resurrect Bussana-Vecchia from the dead, but were soon forced to abandon the idea. In 1963 a group of artists made a renewed attempt: despite fierce protests from the municipality of San Remo, to which the village belongs, they began repairing and restoring the less damaged buildings, and opened several studios and workshops. This former ghost town has now become an international artists' colony.

Below: laundry line, Taggia
Bottom: Bussana-Vecchia

Map
on pages
80–81

7: The Cosmopolitan and the Traditional

San Remo – Ceriana – Baiardo – Apricale – Dolceacqua – Bordighera (50km/30 miles)

Below: beachside hotel, San Remo
Bottom: civic fountain

It was during the 19th century that English lords, Russian tsars and German emperors began spending their winters on the Riviera and tourism was born. The villas, art nouveau hotels and palm-lined sea promenades of San Remo and Bordighera still have a very elegant, cosmopolitan flair of their own. The atmosphere up in the mountain villages, reached from the coast via steep winding roads, is quite different. Peace and quiet reigns, the mountain panoramas are breathtaking, and many of the traditional customs, such as the *Festa della Barca* in Baiardo, date back to pagan times. As a defence measure against the Saracens, several distinctly labyrinthine towns were built in this region over the centuries, one such being the highly atmospheric Dolceacqua.

Allow a day for this route – it'll leave time for a stroll or two through the tiny villages up in the mountains.

SAN REMO

It's surprising that ★★ **San Remo** still hasn't built any kind of monument to the Italian writer Gio-

vanni Ruffini (1807–81). He wasn't one of the greatest names in Italian literature, but he still laid the foundation for the success of the Italian Riviera. His rather kitschy novel *Doctor Antonio*, which he wrote in English and had published in Edinburgh in 1855, is set in San Remo and Bordighera. It was a great success, and several of its readers decided to go and see the Ligurian coast for themselves. The first guests who came to enjoy the mild climate of the Riviera were housed in a private villa belonging to Countess Adele Roverizio di Roccasterone. The Grand Hotel Londra was built in 1860, soon followed by the Royal, still the most exclusive hotel in town today. By the turn of the 20th century there were 25 hotels and around 200 villas; travellers today have a choice of around 250 hotels, campsites and holiday villages, all of differing standards.

Star Attraction
● San Remo

Star resort
Famous residents of San Remo, the most élite of the Riviera's 19th-century winter resorts, included Alfred Nobel, Tchaikovsky and the poet Edward Lear. Lear spent his last years here, dying at Villa Tennyson in 1888. He is buried in the English Cemetery.

THE GOOD OLD DAYS

Although San Remo became a popular destination for modern tourism after World War II, it still likes to remember the good old days when emperors, empresses, tsars and tsarinas all came here, along with princes, dukes, writers and famous artists. The town today has a population of 56,000, and is equipped with the very latest facilities for golf, riding, tennis, sailing, windsurfing and water-skiing; car rallies and sailing regattas of international renown are also held here regularly. All that remains of the *belle époque* these days is the appearance of the place: the grand hotels with their wedding-cake facades, the Corso Imperatrice with its statue of *Spring* draped with garlands, and the elegant villas.

The art nouveau movement has left several impressive traces in San Remo, including the ★ **Villa Nobel**, where Alfred Nobel spent the final years of his life (1891–96). Today it is the seat of the International Institute of Human Rights. Another grand building dating from the turn of the century is of course the **Casino Municipale**. Designed by the French architect Eugène Ferret and built between 1904 and 1906, it earns San

Below: Villa Nobel
Bottom: Casino Municipale

Map on pages 80–81

Sunny events

Records prove that San Remo is the sunniest spot in Liguria. It is also the venue for the Italian Pop Music Festival – an extraordinarily popular event with Italians, held at the end of February. Another popular event takes place in October – the San Remo motor-racing rally. (For more information on the internet: www.rally.sanremo.it)

Remo millions. Rumours have been circulating recently that the casino is being used by the mafia and the *camorra* to launder money, but that hasn't diminished the fascination of such games as *chemin de fer*, roulette and blackjack for its regular clientele. (Opening times: slot machines 10am, 'European Games' 2.30pm. 'American Games' 4.15pm; minimum age 18.)

BISHOP ROMOLO

The name San Remo is synonymous with all that is cosmopolitan. In fact the town should really be known as San Romolo – the name of a small village up in the mountains slightly inland. The Ligurians, who lived here before the Romans arrived, built several forts up on the hilltops around San Remo during the 6th and 5th centuries BC, and when the Romans first reached the Riviera in the 2nd century BC, they founded the town of *Villa Matutiana*, later converted to Christianity by the Genoese bishop Romolo in the 8th century AD. San Romolo then gradually became San Römu.

MAIN SIGHTS

In the town centre

Marking the beginning of the Corso Imperatrice is the impressive Russian Orthodox church of

★**San Basilio** (open Tues, Thur and Sat 3–6.30pm, Sun 9.30am–12.30pm and 3–6.30pm), the construction of which was financed by the Russian 'colony' here during the late 19th century. The large 16th-century Palazzo Borea d'Olmo not only contains a gallery of local art but also the **Civico Museo Archeologico** (open Tues–Sat 9am–noon and 3–6pm, closed Sun and Mon), with its prehistoric collection of finds from the Stone, Bronze and Iron Ages, along with some Roman remains. The other two sections contain a collection of *Risorgimento* memorabilia and paintings, from the 17th to 19th centuries.

The facade of the late Romanesque cathedral of **San Siro** (open daily 7–11.15am and 3–6pm), built in the 13th century above the ruins of a former church on the site, was completely renovated in around 1900. Opposite the left-hand portal with its bas-reliefs is the Battistero, originally a Roman three-aisled church before it was turned into a centralised structure during the 17th century.

FLOWER MARKET

Those planning to stay the night in San Remo should try to get up early and visit one of the daily flower auctions, which start at 5am in the **Mercato dei Fiori** (open Mon–Fri 5–8am for trade only, but observers welcome). San Remo is the largest flower centre in Italy – the glasshouses stretch along the Western Riviera for miles.

OLD TOWN

San Remo has another side, however: the old town of **La Pigna** further uphill, all of it far less elegant and actually rather dilapidated. The attractive jumble of narrow alleyways, flights of steps, vaulted passageways and buttressed houses is mainly inhabited today by the old and the poor of San Remo, Southern Italians working in the flower trade, and also North African immigrants still waiting to be integrated.

The old town is dominated by the richly-decorated baroque pilgrimage church of **Madonna**

Below: San Basilio
Bottom: Old Town alleyway

Map
on pages
80–81

della Costa (17th-century); there's a good view of the gulf and the town from its square.

The old part of San Remo has been neglected for over half a century; local critics regularly complain that similar places in Provence and elsewhere have all been turned into picturesque tourist villages by now. Today, San Remo is turning into one giant old people's home: one third of the population is over 60 years of age, and wealthy pensioners from the neighbouring regions are gradually transforming the town into an Italian version of Florida. In addition, there has been a recent influx of very rich Russians, in true pre-revolutionary tradition, many of whom have moved into the most expensive and exclusive hotels in town.

Below and bottom:
the village of Ceriana

MOUNTAIN VILLAGES

After a detour to the **Pinacoteca e Biblioteca Rambaldi** (open Thur 10am–12.30pm; other times on request, tel: 0184-670131) in **Coldiroldi**, which contains an interesting but rather haphazardly arranged collection of paintings from the 15th to the 19th centuries, and also a valuable library, the route continues out of San Remo and through several well-preserved mountain villages, which illustrate Liguria's 'other' face very successfully.

The first stop on the route is the medieval village of **Ceriana**, distinctive for the way in which its streets are laid out: they follow the natural contours of the steep slope. The village is dominated by the twin-towered parish church of **San Pietro e Paolo**, with a baroque facade; inside there is a polyptych by an anonymous 16th-century artist and a triptych by Francesco Brea dating from 1545. The Romanesque church of Sant'Andrea, with a distinctive spire, contains four Doric columns taken from a pagan temple.

BAIARDO

The mountain village of ★★**Baiardo** (900m/ 2,950ft above sea level) has largely retained its original character, and it comes into its own when the locals celebrate the *Festa della Barca* every Whit Sunday. *Barca* is the Italian word for ship, and the ceremony may date back to pagan times. A tall pole of pine resembling a ship's mast is erected in the square outside the church and decorated with lots of greenery; then a group of folk dancers circle it very slowly, singing a sad song about a lord of Baiardo's daughter who fell in love with a ship's captain.

One well documented tragedy for Baiardo was the severe earthquake of 23 February 1887, when the roof of the church of **San Nicolò** collapsed and over 200 people died. The effects of that tremor can still be observed today in the upper part of the village, where the church ruins bear testimony to the incredible power of the quake. The putti-adorned altar of St Anthony among the ruined walls is a moving sight; mass is still celebrated in front of it.

APRICALE

A few kilometres further along one of those narrow panoramic roads, so typical of the Ligurian hinterland, and ★ **Apricale** comes into view. At the entrance to it there are Gothic gates dating from the 13th century, but Apricale – like many other Ligurian villages these days – is gradually

Star Attraction
● **Baiardo**

👁 **Take a hike**
Experienced hikers should definitely ascend the Monte Bignone (1,299m/4,260ft) behind San Remo. The trip takes 4½ hours, and the view from the top in good weather is quite breathtaking.

Below: Baiardo and (bottom) a view from the town

Map on pages 80–81

becoming depopulated. The main square is especially pretty, with the parish church of **Purificazione di Maria**, rebuilt in the 19th and 20th centuries, and opposite it the Oratorio di San Bartolomeo, with its rococo stucco decoration. The Palazzo del Comune also lies on this piazza; like the other buildings it, too, has contemporary murals depicting rural life and Ligurian landscapes which have earned Apricale the name 'Village of the Artists'. Beyond the former defensive wall is the fortress-like, late medieval church of **Santa Maria degli Angeli**, with its single-aisled interior full of newly-restored fresco cycles dating from the 15th and 18th centuries; the ones depicting the *Assumption* and the *Evangelists* are probably among the oldest. The cemetery church of Sant'Antonio Abate has undergone alteration over the centuries, but still retains a simple Romanesque apse.

Below: Pigna residents and (bottom) the town

PERINALDO

A detour to **Perinaldo** is also a detour away from the remote Ligurian mountains into the world of international science. Giovanni Domenico Cassini was born here in 1625, the first in a long line of astronomers and mathematicians who ran the Paris Observatory for several generations. Cassini's nephew Giacomo Filippo Maraldi was no less illustrious; born in Perinaldo in 1665, he held a top post at the court of Louis XIV, the 'Sun King'. Little wonder that the main street of this long-drawn-out village is named after him, and a local restaurant is called 'Pianeti di Giove' ('Planets of Jupiter'). The placement of the church of **Santuario della Vistiazione** just outside the village is worthy of note: on Cassini's initiative it was aligned with the 'Ligurian line of longitude', and therefore throws no shadow at all on 21 June each year.

ON TO PIGNA

After a series of dizzying mountain hairpins, the route reaches **Isolabona**, down in the valley once more – the Val Nervia, filled with vineyards and olive groves. Instead of driving straight back towards the coast, however, it's well worth heading back into the mountains at this point. Pass the pilgrimage church of **Nostra Signora delle Grazie**, with its unusual 16th-century painting of the family tree of Jesse, and soon the rather unremarkable-looking but culturally very interesting village of **Pigna** comes into view (not to be confused with San Remo's old town, La Pigna). In medieval times, Pigna was situated down in the valley, but was shifted to the hillside above for strategic reasons. The facade of the 15th-century parish church of San Michele is adorned by a magnificent marble rose window, the first ever produced by the Lombard sculptor Giovanni Gagini, many of whose important works can be admired in Genoa. The polyptych inside depicting St Michael is a mature work by the Piedmontese painter Giovanni Canavesio (c 1500), who also executed the grotesque-looking frescoes in the cemetery church of San Bernardino.

Rossese wine
Dolceaqua means literally 'sweet' or 'fresh' water, yet the town is known best for its excellent red wine, redolent of redcurrants and blackberries. This 'Rossese' is regarded by wine buffs as the finest of all the Ligurian DOC wines. In town you can see the production and buy the local wine at Cantina del Rossese, Via Roma 33. Eight kilometres (five miles) north of Dolceaqua is a wine-growing estate where you can purchase both the fine wines and olive oils: Agriturismo Terre Bianche, Arcagna (tel: 0184-31426) – it also has accommodation in eight rooms.

DOLCEACQUA

A much-photographed humpbacked bridge, which fascinated the artist Claude Monet more than 100 years ago, connects the two sections of ★★ **Dolceacqua**. The medieval part, called Terra,

Dolceacqua's medieval bridge

Map
on pages
80–81

on the left bank, makes it clear how Ligurian villages defended themselves against enemy attack at that time: only the locals knew their way through the labyrinth of buildings and passageways, many of which could be bolted shut. On the right bank of the river is the new part, the Borgo. Above the town is a ruined Doria **fortress** in which cultural events are held during the summer months (open daily except Tues 9am–noon and 3–7pm). A modern monument in front of the baroque parish church of **Sant'Antonio** commemorates a local hero, Pier Vincenzo Mela; during the 18th century he discovered how the remains of pressed olives could be turned into oil. The oil sold in Dolceacqua comes from the very best, hand-selected olives, and meals are best accompanied by the delicious local red known as *Rossesse di Dolceacqua*, the third wine in Liguria, alongside *Cinque Terre* and *Colli di Luni*, to have received the coveted DOC qualification.

Below: Dolceacqua
Bottom: exotic plants,
Bordighera

BORDIGHERA

The route now continues via Camporosso back along the coast as far as ★ **Bordighera**. Like San Remo, this town has two sections, both very different: the old town, Alta Bordighera, huddled up on the Capo Sant'Ampelio, once owned by fishermen and farmers, with an excellent view across the coast from the Spianata del Capo; and down in the plain, the elegant, noble, 'garden-city' section, which has given itself up completely to tourism. The 19th-century Municipio (town hall) was designed by Charles Garnier, who also built the Paris Opera House. Bordighera was another popular summer spa resort with the English, and perhaps the most famous member of the town's English colony was the botanist Clarence Bicknell (1842–1918), who was also an Anglican clergyman here. He not only founded the international municipal library but also the ★ **Museo Bicknell** (open Mon–Fri 9.30am–1pm and 1.30–4.45pm), which contains fascinating exhibits, including thousands of prints of the prehistoric cave drawings from Mont Bégo *(see page 102).*

8: Prehistoric Liguria

Ventimiglia – Saorge – La Brigue – Mont Bégo – Tende (50km/31 miles)

Map
on pages
80–81

This route leads across to France's Val de Tende, just next to Liguria, and there are traces of the region's earliest settlers on either side of the border. The mild Riviera climate was already being enjoyed 200,000 years ago in the caves of the Balzi Rossi near Ventimiglia, and between 4,000 and 6,000 years ago people immortalised their daily life and their faith in a series of 45,000 rock drawings in the Vallée des Merveilles, near the French town of Tende.

Below: Ventimiglia Old Town with a view (bottom) over the beach

It's best to allow a full day for this route.

VENTIMIGLIA

Most visitors to **Ventimiglia** spend only very little time there, treating it as a rather chaotic border town that's only worth visiting for its weekly market each Friday. This doesn't do it justice, however: the Old Town, with its jumble of ancient houses to the west of the Roia, and also the newer section to the east of the river, contain a number of interesting sights, as well as remains of the old Roman town.

Ventimiglia's rather gloomy Old Town, with its tall, dark houses and washing hung out to dry on

Map
on pages
80–81

Cave dwellers

Fossils of rhinoceros and elephant alongside marmots, reindeer, and human remains all bear testament to the dwellers of the Balzi Rossi caves, whose history can be traced back 200,000 years. The caves were used as burial chambers in the Upper Paleolithic era, and the connecting cave walkway bearing rock carvings of this time are the only type from this era ever to be found in Northern Italy.

Below: San Michele
Bottom: Area Archeologica

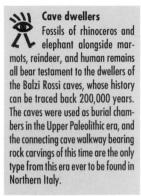

endless lines, is more reminiscent of Southern Italy than the Riviera. It's in these streets, however, that Ventimiglia's most interesting sights can be found.

The ★ **cathedral of Santa Maria Assunta**, for instance, with a crypt full of pre-Romanesque sculpture, or the octagonal baptistry next door to it and the church of **San Michele**, both of which date back to the 11th century; over the centuries they have received various alterations, additions and embellishments.

ARCHAEOLOGICAL SITE

To the east of Ventimiglia is the archaeological site known as **Area Archeologica di Albintimilium**, containing the remains of what was a flourishing Roman community 2,000 years ago. The trapezoid town wall and three town gates dating from around 50BC can still be clearly made out, as can the baths built during the reign of Augustus, and also an amphitheatre from the 2nd century AD, with a seating capacity of 5,000. When it came to strategically important towns, the Romans were always generous with their municipal architecture: the town of *Albintimilium* lay on the trading route to Gaul and Spain, and also on the *Via Julia Augusta*. Several fascinating finds dating from Roman times are on display in the **Museo Civico Archeologico Gerolamo Rossi** in Ventimiglia's Forte dell'Annunziata (open Tues–Fri 9.30am–12.30pm, 3–5pm, Sat and Sun 10am–noon).

CAVES

Go much further back into the past now, however, with a visit to the ★★ **Balzi Rossi caves**, situated at the foot of some red cliffs in Grimaldi, just next to the Franco-Italian border. Excavation work began here in the middle of the 19th century, and towards the end of it Prince Albert I of Monaco decided to finance exploration of a cave which was later named after him – the Grotta del Principe. The skeleton of *Arconthropus* man that was discovered here is thought to be around 240,000 years old.

Three far younger skeletons, of Cro-Magnon men (15,000–30,000 years old), were discovered in the Barma Grande Cave; and the necklaces of sea-shells found in the Grotta dei Fanciulli are highly artistic. The **Museo Preistorico dei Balzi Rossi** (open Tues–Sun 8.30am–7.30pm, caves open until 1 hour before sunset; closed Mon) documents the various fascinating finds from these caves, which are situated right next to the sea.

Star Attraction
● **Balzi Rossi caves**

Below and bottom:
Giardino Hanbury

GIARDINO HANBURY

The Balzi Rossi Museum was founded in 1898 by Thomas Hanbury, a successful British merchant, who is even more famous on the Riviera for his ★ **Giardino Hanbury** (open June–Sept: daily 9.30am–6pm, 7pm mid-June–mid-Sept; Oct-May: daily except Wed 10am–5pm). When he first came here in 1867 to recover from bronchitis, he fell in love with Cape Mortola near Ventimiglia, with its bougainvillea, Aleppo pine, olive and lemon trees, and promptly bought it. He then laid out a botanical garden suitable for exotic plants. At first he was helped by his brother Daniel, who was an experienced botanist.

The gardens slope down towards the sea on a southern slope sheltered from the wind, and cover

Map on pages 80–81

French leave

Part of Italy until 1947, the charming medieval little town of La Brigue (Briga Marittima) is now firmly located in France. As well as being famous for its remarkable frescoes, it is also popular with mountain bikers and hikers.

a vast area. Some 5,000 species of plant from five continents grow here, and 3km (2 miles) of paths, intersecting at the lower end of the gardens with the old Roman *Via Julia Augusta*, lead past palms and agaves, banana and bamboo, Japanese gardens, fruit groves and Australian bush alongside Asian and African exotica.

The Hanbury Gardens are maintained by experts from the University of Genoa; a visit to the small garden café, with a fine view of the coast, rounds off any visit magnificently.

OLD SALT ROAD

The Val Roia begins in Ventimiglia and, despite the fact that it crosses almost 40km (24 miles) of French territory, it's still the best way from Western Liguria to Cuneo and Turin in Piedmont. During the Middle Ages the old salt route led through this valley, connecting the salt-pans in Nice with the Lombardy plain.

Below: Breil-sur-Roya
Bottom: Saorge

To begin with, the villages here are very similar to others in the Ligurian hinterland: the stone houses are all huddled together, and the slopes are covered with ancient, silvery olive-groves. In **Airole**, the grey of the houses contrasts pleasantly with the bright-yellow stuccoed facade of the baroque parish church of **Santi Filippi e Giacomo**, built during the 17th century.

SAN MICHELE

The picturesque and atmospheric hamlet of Fanghetto, right on the French border, with its Romanesque bridge, is actually a part of the village of **San Michele**. The landscape starts getting drier and more alpine now: the olive groves are replaced by forests of larch and pine, and the first large community on French soil is **Breil-sur-Roya** on the left bank of the river.

SAORGE

The adventurously narrow ravine known as the ★ **Gorges de Saorge** has just enough room for one road and a small stream, and at the end of it there's a fascinating view of the magnificently situated mountain village of **Saorge**, high up on the steep slope.

A hike at this point (approx 3 hours) along a much-travelled medieval connecting route between Saorge and the Ligurian village of Pigna *(see page 95)*, leads up to the 1,161-m (3,800-ft) high Passo Muratone. At the top of the pass, the tour along the Franco-Italian border ridge can be extended still further to include the Toraggio-Pietravecchia Massif, with its many caves and the dizzying path known as the Sentiero degli Alpini *(see page 84)*.

Below and bottom: the Gorges de Saorge

LA BRIGUE

The route then leads through the Gorges de Bergue, another ravine with brown-and-green slate walls, to reach **Saint-Dalmas-de-Tende**. Devotees of ecclesiastical art will definitely head straight for the medieval village of **La Brigue** at this point, and visit the pilgrimage church of ★ **Notre-Dame-des-Fontaines**, towering above a romantic gorge.

The church, which was first mentioned in 1375 and is inconspicuous from the outside, contains an artistic treasure which is unique in all the Alps. The Piedmontese painter Giovanni Canavesio,

Below: fresco and portal,
Notre-Dame-des-Fontaines

whose work we already admired in Taggia *(see page 86)* and Pigna *(see page 95)*, painted the interior of this church with several magnificent ★★ **fresco cycles**. A full 320sq m (3,500sq ft) are covered with highly impressive paintings on religious themes, including the *Last Judgement*, the *Passion of Christ* and the *Life of the Virgin*, and in all of them Canavesio adds a realistic, mocking touch of his own. Coincidentally, the fresco cycle was completed on 12 October 1492 – the same day Christopher Columbus discovered America.

MONT BÉGO

Not far away from Notre-Dame-des-Fontaines, to the west of Saint-Dalmas-de-Tende, is a prehistoric cult site. The 2,872-m (9,420-ft) high **Mont Bégo** was considered sacred by Liguria's earliest inhabitants, and the Vallée des Merveilles along its southwestern flank contains around 45,000 ★★ **rock drawings**. Most of them date from the Bronze Age (1800–1500BC), and portray weapons, farmers with ploughs, huts, fields, geometrical figures and also a large number of animals with horns, indicating some kind of ancient fertility cult.

In the summer months shepherds still come up here from the Ligurian coast and from Provence with their flocks, and it was probably their forefathers who drew the sharply stylised figures on the smooth rock-faces in the region.

Much of this primitive art is catalogued in the remarkable prehistoric museum in Bordighera, opened in the 19th century by Clarence Bicknell *(see page 96)*; from 1881 onwards he used to spend many summers up here in a house he built himself in Casterino, on the northwestern slope of Mont Bégo. The region containing the rock drawings has been part of the French national park of Percantour since 1979, and has been classified as a natural site of international importance by UNESCO. Because of vandalism, however, several of the prehistoric drawings can now only be visited in the company of a guide.

VALLÉE DES MERVEILLES

From the Lac des Mesces (1,375m/4,500ft above sea level) which can be reached by car from Saint-Dalmas-de-Tende, the **Vallée des Merveilles** is another 2½ hours on foot. The valley is open – weather permitting – from June to mid-October. The most famous drawing in this 'valley of miracles' is the so-called *Chef de Tribu* ('tribal chieftain'), and unlike many others it can be touched – because it's a copy, and the original is safe and well in the museum near Tende *(see box)*.

TENDE

Tende is an old and appealing trading town, dominated by the ruins of a medieval castle destroyed by French troops in 1691. Many of the houses in the centre have sculpted portals with inscriptions dating from the 15th and 16th centuries. The main portal of the cathedral of **Nôtre-Dame de l'Assomption**, which was consecrated in 1518, is particularly fine. Masons from the Ligurian village of Cenova cut these reliefs of the *Assumption*, the *Annunciation* and *Christ with the Twelve Apostles* from greenish-grey serpentine – a good example of the kind of 'cultural exchange' that has been going on among the French and Italian speakers of this border region for centuries.

Star Attractions
● fresco cycles
● rock drawings, Mont Bégo

Ancient stones
The 'Vale of Marvels' is an extraordinarily scenic Alpine part of the Parc National du Mercantour, which is famous for the Neolithic to Iron-Age stone carvings hewn into the slopes of Mont Bégo. For visitor information on the Vale of Marvels (Valle delle Meraviglie – or Vallée des Merveilles), tel: 0033 493 047 371. Just outside Tende, the Musée des Merveilles (open winter: 10am– 5pm & until 6.30pm in summer (no more late-night opening on Sat), closed Tues) is well worth a visit. Here are showcased finds from prehistoric to Roman times and rock carvings from Mont Bégo.

Sunset in Tende

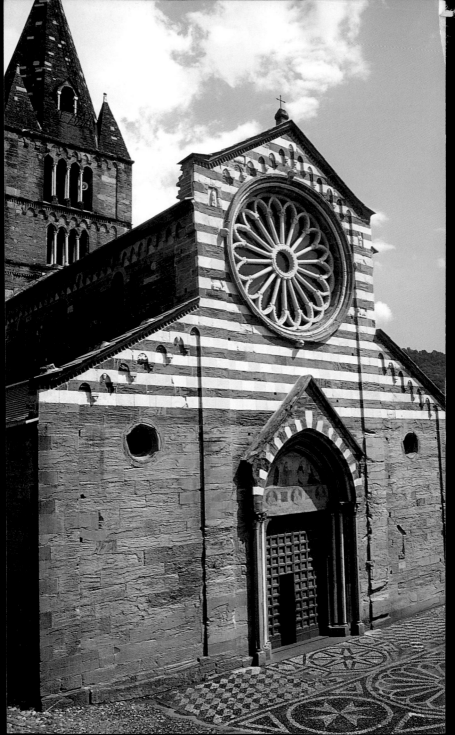

Art and Architecture

The oldest artefacts in Liguria (5,000–6,000 years old) are the cave paintings on Mont Bégo. They aren't easy to reach, however: the caves lie on French territory and are at the end of a long mountain hike. The mysterious stelae from Lunigiana, not far from Liguria, date from the Bronze Age and can be admired in La Spezia's museum.

> **Prehistor...**
> Neanderthal ...
> the Ligurian a...
> the Ice Age some 50,000 y...
> The caves of Balzi Rossi *(see p...*
> represent one of Italy's ...
> important prehistoric sites. The c...
> dwellings at Toirano *(see page 74,*
> and Finale *(see page 73)* are also
> impressive.

ROMAN REMAINS

The old Roman road from Albenga to Alassio is a monument to Roman engineering. There are also five Roman bridges in the Val Ponci near Finale, and the ruins of some villas in Bussana and San Remo. The best preserved structure, however, is in Ventimiglia: the Roman *Albintimilium*. Luni also has a forum, a temple of Diana, and the villas Casa dei Mosaici and Casa degli Affreschi, all of them bearing testimony to the former might of the Romans' 'marble harbour'; cultural events are still staged in the amphitheatre today.

Left: Basilica dei Fieschi, Lavagna
Below: stelae from Lunigiana
Bottom: Albenga cathedral

MEDIEVAL

Important works of medieval art and architecture, of which there are many, include the early Christian baptistry and cathedral in Albenga, the Basilica dei Fieschi in Lavagna and the Abbazia di Borzone inland from it, the baptistry and church of San Michele in Ventimiglia, the monasteries of San Domenico in Taggia and San Fruttuoso di Capodimonte near Portofino, as well as the churches of San Paragorio in Noli and San Pietro in Portovenere.

GOTHIC TO RENAISSANCE

During the 15th century the Dominican monastery in Taggia became a bastion of Gothic painting, and there are several Renaissance features too; the two main artists involved here were Giovanni Canavesio and Ludovico Brea. At the same time, stonemasons provided countless palazzi and churches with magnificently carved Gothic slate portals; there's hardly a town or village without one.

The rather provincial history of art in Liguria was brightened up a lot by the Florentine painter Perin del Vaga, who provided Genoa's Palazzo Doria with its magnificent frescoes; his successor Luca Cambiaso (1527–85) influenced generations of 17th- and 18th-century artists, including Bernardo Strozzi, Domenico Piola, Bernardo Castello, and Gregorio and Lorenzo de Ferrari.

RENAISSANCE VILLAS

The exceptionally mild climate of Genoa encouraged wealthy families to build splendid villas in or near the city. When these private villas became public property, they were a real discovery, not least because many of them are surrounded by magnificent parks and gardens.

It was back in the mid-16th century that Galeazzo Alessi, an Umbrian-born architect trained in Rome, arrived in Genoa and, with his Renaissance Villa Giustiani-Cambiaso, provided the basis for countless more town palazzi and country villas that were built during the two centuries that followed; these include the splendid Villa Serra in Sant'Ilario, surrounded by one of the prettiest parks in all Italy, and the famous Villa Gropallo in Nervi. The Villa Durazzo Pallavicini in the west of Genoa is described as the pearl among the villas of Liguria.

GENOESE BAROQUE

By the early 17th century, Genoa had attracted such Flemish masters as Peter Paul Rubens and Van Dyck, who produced magnificent works of art for the city. For some, Rubens' painting *Cirumcision* (1605), for the high altar of Genoa's church Ss. Ambrogio e Andrea, is considered to be the history of art's first Baroque painting. Fame spread, and Liguria became the home of some splendid picture collections, many of which are now in private hands. Yet it is still possible to see masterpieces by many, including Rubens and Van Dyck, Titian, Tintoretto, Caravaggio and Veronese, in Genoa's public art galleries, including the Palazzi Rosso, Reale and newly restored Palazzo Bianco.

LATER DEVELOPMENTS

A new construction boom began when the Riviera was discovered by foreign tourists in the second half of the 19th century. Europe's classical roots were being rediscovered, and so a number of elaborate neoclassical buildings appeared. Many can be seen along the Western Riviera (note those by Charles Garnier, architect of Monte Carlo's casino, in Bordighera). The end of the century saw art nouveau creeping in.

Memorable modern buildings include the railway station in Savona, designed in 1960 by gifted Italian architect, Pier Luigi Nervi. Other 20th century architectural monuments in Genoa have not been uncontroversial. The Carlo Felice Theatre, bombed during World War II, remained closed until 1987, when rebuilding began; whilst its highly sophisticated stage machinery has earned it many accolades, the futuristic design is not to everyone's taste. Re-opened to coincide with the Great Columbus Celebration Expo in 1992, Renzo Piano's redevelopment of Genoa's old port did much to breathe new life into the region's capital and continued in celebration of Genoa's status as European City of Culture in 2004.

Below: Palazzo Reale, Genoa
Centre: art nouveau,
San Remo
Bottom: neoclassical villa,
Santa Margherita

Literature and Music

This, Italy's most forested region, was also always known as the land of remote fishing villages under blue skies and restless seas. But it exercised a huge draw over the English and American 'litterati' of the 19th to 20th century. Percy Bysshe Shelley and his wife Mary lived on the bay of Lerici, where he spent his last months before his drowning accident in 1822. Other regular visitors to Liguria included Nietzsche, Maupassant, Goethe, Hemingway, Byron, Ezra Pound and W.B. Yeats. The master of 'nonsense verse', Edward Lear, spent his last years at San Remo, and before him Charles Dickens made Genoa a base for his travels in Italy in 1844.

Below: Shelley memorial, La Spezia
Bottom: local bookstall

Wagner frequented the eastern shores of Liguria, while the Russian colony in San Remo attracted such luminaries as Tchaikovsky, who composed both the Fourth Symphony and Eugene Onegin while staying here in 1878.

The Muretto in Alassio, where the autographs of some of the great movers and shakers are etched in the ceramic tiles – from the likes of Ernest Hemingway to Louis Armstrong – illustrates the appeal of the Riviera.

Ligurian home-grown talent includes Eugenio Montale, born in Genoa in 1896 *(see page 50)*. In 1975, he won the Nobel Prize in Literature.

Festival Calendar

For full details of the numerous festivals held in the region, contact the tourist office *(see page 119)* or try www.italiantourism.com

January 20 Festival of St Sebastian in Dolceacqua and Camporosso; a decorated laurel tree is carried through the town.

Easter Processions held in Ceriana on Maundy Thursday and Good Friday, and in Savona and Triora on Good Friday.

May Second Sunday The *Sagra del Pesce* ('Fish Festival') in Camogli; vast amounts of fish are fried in an enormous frying pan and distributed among guests for free.

Whit Sunday The *Festa della Barca* ('Boat Festival') in Baiardo; ritual dance around a tree-trunk, thought to date from pagan fertility rituals.

Sunday after Corpus Christi *Infiorata* in Diano Marina and Sassello; the streets are strewn with thousands of multi-coloured flower petals.

June 24 Festival of St John in Genoa; street procession and holiday to celebrate the patron saint.

July 1–3 *Nostra Signora di Montallegro* in Rapallo; procession and firework display.

July/August International Festival of Chamber Music, held in the delightful village of Cervo.

August First Sunday *Stella Maris* in Camogli; atmospheric boat procession.

Palio del Golfo in La Spezia. Festival on the water with regatta and fireworks.

Corteo Storico in Ventimiglia; procession in period costumes to commemorate an historical event.

August 13–14 *Torta dei Fieschi* in Lavagna; festival commemorating medieval *fieschi* weddings, with a giant cake, tournaments and a procession.

August 23 *Cristo degli Abissi* in San Fruttuoso; divers descend to a bronze statue of Christ lying on the ocean floor.

September *Sagra della Lumaca* ('Snail Festival') in Molini di Triora; in celebration of the snail.

September Second Sunday *Regata dei Rioni* in Noli; regatta with historical procession.

December 13 *Santa Lucia* in Toirano; festival with a torchlight procession.

Everyone joins in
All Italians love festivals. Whether it is a religious occasion, a chance to glorify the bounty of the sea or forests in a gourmet *sagra*, or simply a reason for staging a big party or parade, everyone is always welcome to join in. Liguria excels especially in Easter processions, the most celebrated of which is that held on Good Friday at Savona. There are many festivals in recognition of this, including the famous Festa della Barca on Whit Sunday at Baiardo, and the fried fish *sagra* at Camogli on the second Sunday in May. In mid October, Genoa hosts the International Boat Show – the largest in the Mediterranean.

Diano Marina festival

FOOD AND DRINK

Ligurian cooking is country cooking. The numerous Riviera restaurants with varied seafood dishes do little to reflect the fact that genuine Ligurian cuisine is influenced markedly more by the land than by the sea.

PESTO AND FOCACCIA

The main ingredient of *trenette con pesto*, the Ligurians' favourite dish, is basil, a herb long a staple of local cuisine (mariners used it as protection against scurvy and similar diseases). The *pesto* sauce also contains grated cheese, garlic and olive oil, and is poured over flat noodles or lasagne. *Ceci* are also vital in local cooking: small, yellow chick-peas, which came from the Orient. They provide the basis for two vegetable soups, *mesciua* and *zimino di ceci*, as well as for two classics of Ligurian cuisine, the *panissa* and the *farinata*. A *panissa* is a kind of chick-pea paste cut into slices and fried in oil, and the *farinata* is a thin pancake made of chick-pea flour sold at traditional 'Farinotti' establishments. The mainstay of the 'humble' Genovese cuisine is *focaccia* – the dough, which is soft yet crispy, plain yet tasty, flavoured simply with olive oil and salt – eaten simply when you feel like it.

MAIN COURSES

Popular main courses (*secondi*) include salted quiches, most famously the multi-layered *torta pasqualina*, with vegetables, eggs and other ingredients. Ligurian housewives and cooks pride themselves on their vegetables stuffed with various (vegetarian) ingredients, such as onions, aubergines, tomatoes or peppers. Creating a *cappon magro* requires time and patience: it is a pyramid consisting of six or seven different kinds of cooked fish with lots of different vegetables, and is decorated with shrimps, oysters and other crustaceans. The dish has to be ordered in advance. As far as meat is concerned, chicken dishes tend to predominate; the seafood dishes very often feature sardines and stockfish. A speciality is 'buridda alla genovese' – luxurious fish soup or stew containing mussels, shrimps, octopus, squid and clams. The main reason why Ligurian cuisine is so delicious is the subtle mixture of fresh herbs – especially marjoram, oregano and basil.

DOLCI

Traditional sweets include *pandolce* – a delicious type of fruit loaf with succulent raisins, *sfogliate* – puff pastries from Varigotti – and *cobaita* – honey-coated pieces of hazelnut and nougat from Ventimiglia. You will also find *baci* everywhere: nut-filled chocolates.

Restaurants

The following selection, from the region's most popular destinations, are

---

Ligurian wines

A good meal deserves a good wine, of which there is no shortage in Liguria. From what is regarded as probably the finest, the deliciously rich red Rossese of Dolceaqua, to the famous white, apricot-flavoured Sciacchetrà from the Cinque Terre, there are 20 wines that have been awarded the DOC accolade (*denominazione d'origine controllato*). Other noteworthy wines include Pigato, Vermentino del Ponente, Bianco di Gavi, Cinque Terre whites and, if you prefer red wines, Barbera of Dolcetto. Even if some of the local wines have not yet attained the DOC label, they are nonetheless very drinkable and are excellent accompaniments to the local Ligurian cuisine.

listed according to three categories: €€€ = expensive, €€ = medium-priced and € = inexpensive.

Alassio

Palma, Via Cavour 11, tel: 0182-640 314; closed Wed & Nov. Located in the centre of Alassio, an excellent one-Michelin-star restaurant, family-run. Fresh fish and home-squeezed extra virgin olive oil a speciality. €€€.

Sail Inn, Via Brennero, 34, tel: 0182-640 232; closed Mon & 6 Jan–6 Mar. Popular & near beach; fresh seafood a speciality. €€.

Albissola Marina

Al Cambusiere, Via Repetto 86, tel: 019-481663; closed Mon & two weeks in Jan. Located in heart of old town in a lovely 17th-century building. Specialities are fresh seafood and fish. €€.

La Familiare, Piazza del Popolo 8, tel: 019-489 480; closed Nov. Genuine Ligurian cuisine: seafood/fish the speciality. Tables outside in summer. €€.

Ameglia

Paracucchi-Locanda dell'Angelo, Strada Sarazana-Marinella, Viale XXV Aprile 60, tel: 0187-64391; closed Mon and 7–28 Jan. Established restaurant linked to a hotel. Excellent, gastronomic temple since 1970s. €€€.

Dai Pironcelli, Montemarcello (5km/3 miles from Ameglia), Via delle Mura 45, tel: 0187-601 252; closed Wed & June–Sept lunch. Local fish and meat dishes; charming and efficient service. €€.

Arma di Taggia

La Conchiglia, Via Lungomare 33, tel: 0184-43169; closed Wed & Thur lunchtime, 2 weeks in both June & Nov. Must book. Old fishermen's house by the sea; charming atmosphere, gourmet Ligurian cuisine (holds one Michelin star). €€€.

Borgio Verezzi

Da Casetta, Piazza San Pietro 12, tel: 019-610 166; closed Tues and lunch except Sat–Sun & festivals. Advise booking. Fine Ligurian food beneath vaulted ceiling; lovely garden. €€.

Doc, Via Vittorio Veneto 1, tel: 019-611 477; closed Mon, Tues & lunch except Sat & Sun. Popular, gracious fish restaurant; *tortino di cioccolato* and *torta di mele* also specialities; excellent wine list. €€€.

Camogli

Rosa, Largo Casabona 11, tel: 0185-773 411; closed Tues & Wed lunch. Also 10 Jan–15 Feb, 14 Nov–6 Dec. Fine old house overlooking the sea. Delicious specialities are fresh seafood and classic Ligurian cuisine. €€–€€€.

Vento Ariel, Calata Porto, tel: 0185-771 080; closed Wed. Excellent seafood on the harbour front. €€–€€€.

Camporosso

Gino, Camporosso Mare, Via Braie 10, tel: 0184-291 493; closed Tues (Mon in July & Aug; open eves only in July & Aug). Family-run, elegant & popular; Ligurian cuisine. €€€.

Manuel, Corso Italia, 265, tel/fax 0184-205037. Elegant, family-run, near the sea. Must book. Closed Mon & Tues lunch. €€.

Cinque Terre

Cappun Magru, Via Volastra 19, Groppo (3km/2 miles from Manarola), tel: 0187-920563; closed Mon, Tues and lunchtime except Sun and 10 Dec–10 Feb. Must book. Small and welcoming in a private house specialising in the food of the Levante. €€.

Gambero Rosso, Piazza G. Marconi 7, Vernazza, tel: 0187-812 265; closed Mon (except in summer) and Jan & Feb. Classic restaurant set in pretty piazza; speciality is the freshest seafood, served with good wines. €€€.

Marina Piccola, Via Lo Scalo 16, Manarola, tel:0187-920 103; closed Tues & Nov. Stunning sea views and delicious regional dishes that specialise in the fruits of the sea. €€.

Dolceacqua

Gastone, Piazza Garibaldi 2, tel: 0184-206 577; closed Mon eve and Tues & 2 weeks in Oct. Near the castle; serves rabbit and lamb dishes as well as seafood. €–€€.

Finalborgo

Ai Torchi, Via dell'Annunziata 12, tel: 019-690 531; closed Tues (except Aug) and 7 Jan–10 Feb. Booking advised. Elegance and good seafood in a former 16th-century oil-mill. €€.

Genoa

La Bitta Nella Pergola, Via Casaregis 52r, tel: 010-588 543; closed Sun eve and Mon, also 1–7 Jan and 8–31 Aug. Must book. Excellent, traditional seafood cuisine. This is an elegant and much acclaimed restaurant with one Michelin star. €€€.

Gran Gotto, Viale Brigate Bisagno 69r, tel: 010-564 344; closed Sun and Sat lunch and 11–29 Aug. Widely considered one of Genoa's best restaurants, there is a strong emphasis on seafood, but carnivores are well catered for – as are chocoholics. €€€.

Trattoria da Rina, Via Mura delle Grazie 3r, tel: 010-246 6475; closed Mon and Aug. Excellent fish restaurant near harbour. Established since 1945: Genoa's oldest restaurant. €€.

Imperia

Al Gambero, Borgo Marina via Scarincio 16/18, tel: 0183-667 413; closed Mon and 10–31 Jan. Lovely location overlooking the sea. Specialities include Ligurian dishes and seafood. €€.

Lanterna Blu da Tonino, Via Scarincio,32, tel: 0183 638 59; closed Wed lunch in summer. Overlooking the harbour; tastefully furnished; specialises in freshest fish and seafood. €€€.

La Spezia

Il Ristorantino di Bayon, Via Felice Cavallotti, 23, tel: 0187 732 209; closed Sun. Atmospheric & rustic; in the heart of old town. Fish and meat specialities. Covers limited: booking advised. €€.

Il Sogno di Angelo, Via del Popolo 39, tel: 0187 514 041; closed Sun, last 2 weeks in Aug & 1 week in Jan. Must book. Creative, gastronomic cuisine; emphasis on fine seafood. Deservedly popular. €€€.

Dining out in Portofino

Lavagna
Martin Pescatore, Via del Cigno 1, Cavi (3km/2 miles from Lavagna), tel: 0185-390 026; closed June–Sept lunchtime except Sat/Sun; Oct–May Fri–Sun. Overlooks beach; specialities: seafood and excellent Ligurian cuisine. Extensive wine list. €€–€€€.

Pigna
Terme, Via Madonna Assunta Sud-Est, tel: 0184-241 046; closed Wed except Aug; Nov–Mar dinner only on reservation. Home-cooked traditional specialities; restaurant with rooms. €.

Portofino
Ca' Peo, Via dei Caduti 80 (half hour drive from Portofino in Chiavari a Leivi), tel: 0185-319 696, closed Mon and Tues lunch. Booking essential. Delicious Ligurian food and wine. Highly acclaimed. €€€.
Da Puny, Piazza Martiri dell'Olivetta 5, tel: 0185-269 037; closed Thur & mid-Dec–mid-Feb. Good, traditional fish and seafood by the harbour. €€€.
Taverna del Marinaio, Piazza Martiri dell'Olivetta 36; tel: 0185 269 103; closed Tues. Harbour setting; tables outside; excellent seafood. €€€.

Portovenere
Trattoria La Marina-da Antonio, Piazza Marina 6, tel: 0187-790686; closed Thur and Nov. Pleasant, family-run, traditional trattoria on the port specializing in fresh fish. €€.
Taverna del Corsaro, Calata Doria 102, tel: 0187-790 622; closed Mon in alternate months. Excellent seafood;, located in medieval tower by sea. €€.

Rapallo
U Giancu, Via San Massimo 78 , San Massimo (3km/2 miles from Rapallo), tel: 0185-260 505. Original cartoons on the walls. Ligurian cooking with vegetarian options. Impressive garden. €€.

San Remo
Le Cantine Sanreminesi, Via Palazzo 7, tel: 0184-572 063; closed Sun. Centrally located wine cellar; good typical dishes and snacks. €.
Paolo e Barbara, Via Roma 47, tel: 0184-531 653; closed Wed and Thur; 19–30 Dec, 23–29 Jan & 22 June–7 July. Book. One-star Michelin restaurant: highly imaginative food. €€€.

Santa Margherita Ligure
L'Approdo da Felice, Via Cairoli 26, tel: 0185-281 789; closed Mon, Tues lunch, 10–27 Dec and Mar. Traditional Ligurian specialities with emphasis on seafood. Pleasant, shady garden. €€.
Trattoria Cesarina, Via Mameli 2/c, tel: 0185-286 059; closed Tue, 20 Dec–Jan and lunchtime in July and Aug. Good, traditional Ligurian cuisine in this friendly trattoria. Very pleasant surroundings in the historical centre. €€.

Savona
L'Arco Antico, Piazza Lavagnola 26r, tel: 019-820 938; closed Sun and for 10 days in Jan and Sept. Open for dinner (lunch reservation only). Creative seafood cuisine in this award-winning little restaurant, which has one Michelin star. €€€.
Molo Vecchio, Via Baglietto 8r, tel: 019-854 219; closed Tues and 2 weeks in Sept. Inventive Ligurian cuisine in the old quarter of town. €€–€€€.

Sestri Levante
Fiammenghilla Fieschi, Via Pestella 6 (Trigoso 1½km/1 mile), tel: 0185-481 041; closed Mon & lunch Tues–Fri & 2 weeks Oct–Nov & 2 weeks Jan–Feb. Must book. Excellent cuisine and service in a 17th-century palazzo. €€.
Portobello, Via Portobello 16, tel: 0185-41566; closed Wed (except July and Aug), Jan–23 Feb and 3 Nov–Dec. By bay; summer service on beach; specialities: fish & seafood. €€–€€€.

ACTIVE HOLIDAYS

The Riviera is a paradise for swimmers and mountain climbers alike. There's a vast range of activities on offer for the actively inclined.

GOLF

There are five idyllically situated golf courses in Liguria. Two 9-hole courses are located in Arenzano, in the province of Genoa, and in Marigola near Lerici (province of La Spezia); the three 18-hole courses are at Garlenda (province of Savona), Rapallo (province of Genoa) and San Remo (province of Imperia). For more information contact the Federazione Italiana Golf (FIG), Comitato Regionale Liguria, Piazza Rossetti 5/9, I-16129 Genoa, tel: 010-592 410, or visit www.federgolf.it/circoli.asp.

HIKING AND MOUNTAIN-CLIMBING

The Italians are increasingly interested in hiking; new routes are being opened in the Ligurian Alps and Apennines. For long-distance walkers, the *Alta Via dei Monti Liguri (see box)*, which runs the length of the Ligurian Apennines, offers a wonderful opportunity to sample the different landscapes of the region. Mountain climbers will find what they're looking for in Pietravecchia, around Albenga and near Finale Ligure. The scenic Cinque Terre are also excellent walking terrains with trails to suit all abilities.

Contact Club Alpino Italiano (CAI), Piazza Palermo 11, I-16129 Genoa, tel: 010-310 584, www.cai.it.

RIDING

Horse-riding is increasingly popular in Liguria. The hills and mountains inland provide many opportunities for day trips or treks lasting several days.

For more information, contact the Associazione Nazionale per il Turismo Equestre (ANTE), Vico Campetto 10, I-16123 Genoa, tel: 010-291 419.

SAILING

The Ancient Romans and the Ligurians were just as pleased as today's sailors to discover the many excellent mooring locations along the Riviera, and today the marinas and yachting harbours contain all the modern conveniences. Dinghies as well as motorboats are available for hire at the

The Alta Via

The very well-marked hiking route known as the Alta Via dei Monti Liguri begins at the coast close to Ventimiglia, runs the length of the Ligurian Apennines, and ends around 440km (270 miles) further on at Ceparana, north of La Spezia. The longest hiking route on Italian soil, it is divided into 44 different sections, each between 5km (3 miles) and 17km (10 miles) long, and covers differences in elevation of up to 952m (3,120ft). The highest point of the Alta Via is the summit of Monte Saccaretto (2,200m/7,220ft) on the Franco-Italian border.

What makes this Ligurian hiking route so special is the sheer wealth of natural scenery along the way, the fascinating difference between the Mediterranean landscape on one side and the Alpine one on the other, and also the fact that many sections of it follow ancient medieval trading routes. It therefore leads through remote Ligurian mountain villages that are gradually being depopulated, and past the imposing ruins of several old fortified sites that were so essential in this strategically disputed region. Don't worry about not being fit enough, or good enough at trekking: there are villages dotted every few miles along the route.

resorts. More information can be obtained from the Federazione Italiana Vela, Comitato Regionale, Viale Brigato Bisagno 2/17, I-16129 Genoa, tel: 010-589 431.

SURFING

Surfing is possible in almost every resort, and schools and board hire are available in most places. The local tourist information offices *(see page 119)* can provide more information.

SWIMMING

The 317-km (197-mile) coast has no shortage of great places to swim, but only a few beaches are freely accessible. This is partly due to the fact that many hotels own their own beach, and partly because there are no less than 460 *stabilimenti balneari*, or 'bathing areas', which are cordoned off stretches of beach that can only be entered on payment of an admission charge. They can be anything from beautiful bays to long sand or pebble beaches ideal for children.

Anyone looking for peace and quiet should head for the rocky part of the coast for a swim; remember, though, that it's not all that easily accessible.

*Windsurfing
at Breil-sur-Roya*

Broadly, the beaches can be divided into two separate types in Liguria. The Levante – or eastern section – tends to have pebbles, while the western Ponente area has sandy beaches. Overall, the quality is good and there are many EU blue flags flying, denoting clean and well-manicured beaches. The Blue Flag Awards, presented annually, show good environmental standards, sanitary and safety facilities at beaches and marinas.

The waters are also popular for scuba divers, especially around Santa Margherita *(see page 43)*.

WINTER SPORTS

Believe it or not, it is possible to ski in Liguria, despite the mild Riviera climate. The region has three winter sports areas, catering for many different kinds of activity: Alberola, near Sassello in the province of Savona, on the northern slope of Monte Beigua (1,287m/4,220ft); Monesi di Triora (province of Imperia), on the Monte Saccarello (2,200m/7,220ft); and last but not least, Santo Stefano d'Aveto (province of Genoa), the best-equipped skiing centre in Liguria.

More information on skiing is available from Club Alpino Italiano (CAI), Piazza Palermo 11, I-16129 Genoa, tel: 010-310 584, or www.liguriasci.it.

PRACTICAL INFORMATION

Getting There

BY PLANE

The only international airport in Liguria is Christopher Columbus Airport in Genoa, 7km (4 miles) from the city (www.airport.genova.it). British Airways flies twice a day from Gatwick, with a flying time of 1 hour 50 minutes. Contact **British Airways** Linkline on tel: 0345-222111; in the US 1-800-AIR-WAYS. For cheaper flights to Genoa, you can try **Ryanair** who fly out from Stansted Airport. Contact www.ryanair.com, or tel: 0870-1569 569 (UK) or 01-609 7800 (Dublin).

All Alitalia flights involve a change in Rome to join the regular daily connecting services to Genoa. If not flying via London, American passengers should fly into Rome to make the connection. **Alitalia**: in London, tel: 08705-448 259; New York 212-582 8900; Los Angeles tel: 310-568 0901.

There is a regular bus service called Volabus from Genoa Airport to the city centre, which calls at the two train stations and takes about 30 minutes.

You can also fly to Nice, in the south of France, which is just 48 km (30 miles) from San Remo. Easyjet (www.easyjet.com, tel: 0870-6000 000) have flights to Nice at very competitive prices. Other airlines include BMI Baby (www.bmibaby.com, tel: 0870 264 2229, Flybe (www.flybe.com, tel 0870 567 4564). Volare Airlines: (www.volare-airlines.com, tel: 01293 562266) and MyTravelLite (www.mytravellite.com, tel: 0870 156 4564).

BY RAIL

Liguria is served by international train services from Nice, Mont Cenis Gotthard, Germany and Austria. If travelling direct from the UK, take the Eurostar to Gare du Nord in Paris, then cross to Gare du Lyon for the overnight 21.14 to Genoa. Call Rail Europe on tel: 08705-300 003; www.raileurope.co.uk Many trains travel on from Genoa to Ventimiglia in the west or La Spezia in the east.

BY BUS

There are no direct bus services, but Eurolines operate services from London to Milan, where the excellent regional bus services can be used. An alternative would be to take a bus to Milan and then a 2-hour train ride.

BY ROAD

There are good motorways all across France, and depending on which route is taken, the passes from France or Switzerland into Italy connect easily to the *autostrada* in Liguria. The Mont Blanc Tunnel and the Great St Bernard Tunnel are among those open year-round (but check before leaving). Tolls are charged on French and Italian motorways.

> **Swiss diversion**
> Drivers contemplating travelling to Italy via Switzerland should bear in mind that they need a *vignette*, an annual road pass, costing around £18 and available at the border or at Swiss tourist offices.

BY BOAT

Genoa's harbour is not only the biggest in Italy, it is also the most important port of call for both passengers and cargo in the whole of the Mediterranean. Ships sail here from the ports of Europe, America, Africa and the other continents. It is served by Mediterranean ferry services (from Sardinia, Sicily, Corsica, Barcelona and Tunisia; www.onlineferries.com), and here are regular sailings along the coast to La Spezia, Savona and Imperia. In recent years, cruise holidays have become increasingly popular and, thanks to the modern facilities available, Genoa has become a popular point of departure for cruise ships.

Getting Around

MOTORISTS

A national driving licence and country stickers suffice, though a green insurance card is recommended. Breakdown service is usually free of charge for members of automobile clubs. Seatbelts are compulsory in Italy. Never leave anything in the car which might attract thieves – not even for a few moments. Also, remember that the fines for traffic offences in Italy (parking, overtaking, speed limits, etc) are very high. The following speed limits apply to motor traffic in Italy unless otherwise indicated: 50kmph (30mph) in built-up areas, 90kmph (55mph) on country roads, and 130kmph (75mph) on motorways *(autostrada)*. Speed limits are often lowered at weekends or on public holidays. Police checks have become much stricter in recent

Two-tier train at
Riomaggiore, Cinque Terre

times, and excessive speed as well as excessive alcohol consumption can cost motorists their licence – this also applies to foreign drivers. The breakdown number of the Automobile Club Italiano is 116. For emergency numbers, see page 121.

> **Filling up**
> Remember that, like most of the rest of Italy, petrol stations tend to close for lunch; cash-operated filling stations run on €5 notes. For garages that stay open at night, ask at your hotel. Also, be sure to have enough petrol before heading into the mountains.

BY BUS

The buses in Liguria are indispensable for reaching the more remote villages. Major centres have their own local bus services as well as firms operating long-distance and regional routes.

BY TRAIN

One ideal and green way to avoid all the queues on the coast roads is simply to take the train. The service is good but because trains tend to be popular and crowded travellers who haven't booked in advance should arrive at the station at least 30 minutes before departure.

The rail network mirrors that of the motorway. The main Ventimiglia–La Spezia line serves travellers from Northern Italy arriving from Milan and Turin via Genoa, and connects with the Tyrrenhian Line to and from Rome and Southern Italy. Rapid travel is guaranteed by TEE, EC and IC trains, with conveniently timed connections to all destinations. But there are also slower trains operating along the Ligurian coast, stopping frequently along the route.

There are two stations in Genoa. Principe is the terminal for trains from France, Turin, Milan and Rome. Brignole serves the local lines. The Italian State Railways offer a variety of fare reductions. For information on these and departure times, enquire at the local railway stations.

DISABLED TRAVELLERS

Whilst facilities are generally not especially prevalent in Italy, they are certainly improving. Do check beforehand on availability of wheelchair ramps in museums and galleries. There are reserved seats at the front of trams and buses, but it is as well to try to travel outside peak periods as they can be difficult to gain access to at these times. In general, Italians will always try to be helpful, especially if you alert the hotel or restaurant to your needs beforehand by phone. If you need to bring a guide or hearing dog, contact your nearest consulate or embassy for details on how to proceed.

Facts for the Visitor

TRAVEL DOCUMENTS

Visitors from European Union countries require either a passport or identification card to enter Italy. Holders of passports from most other countries do not usually require visas for a period not exceeding three months.

Visitors bringing their own car will need the vehicle registration documents and insurance certificates.

CUSTOMS

There have been practically no customs limits for nationals of EU member states since 1993. The following are just rough guidelines: 800 cigarettes, 200 cigars, 1kg of tobacco, 90 litres of wine. Citizens of non-EU member states can bring in 400 cigarettes, one bottle of spirits, two of wine, 50g of perfume. Unlimited amounts of foreign currency and euros may be brought in and out of Italy, but need to be declared if the sum exceeds €10,500.

TOURIST INFORMATION

Here are two addresses for the Italian Tourist Office (ENIT):

In the UK: 1 Princes Street, London W1R 9AY, tel: 020-7408 1254, 020-7355 1557, fax: 020-7493 6695, email: enitlond@globalnet.co.uk website: www.enit.it

In the US: 630 Fifth Avenue, Suite 1565, New York NY 10111, tel: 212-245 4822, fax: 212-586 9249, email: enitny@italiantourism.com website: www.italiantourism.com

Other useful websites to look at are www.enit.it/uk and www.itwg.com

Liguria: When in Liguria, contact the SRPT (Servizio Regionale di Promozione Turistica), Via Fieschi 15, I-16121 Genoa, tel: 010-548 4818, fax: 010-541 046.

CURRENCY AND EXCHANGE

In 2002, the euro (EUR) became the official currency used in Italy. Notes are denominated in 5, 10, 20, 50, 100 and 500 euros; coins in 1 and 2 euros and 1, 2, 5, 10, 20 and 50 cents. Lire are no longer considered legal currency in Italy.

Most credit cards, including Visa, Access and American Express, are ccepted in hotels, restaurants and shops and for air and train tickets and cash at any bank. All the larger towns in Liguria have cash machines ('Bancomat').

TIPPING

A tip is generally given for good service in restaurants, even when the service is already included *(servizio compreso)*; however, the amount is never as generous as 10 per cent. It is customary to leave a few coins in bars and cafés, and give around €1 to people such as taxi drivers, doormen, porters and chambermaids.

BILLS AND RECEIPTS

Not only the Italians themselves but also foreign tourists are expected to have receipts *(ricevuta fiscale)* made out by restaurants, hotels, car repair workshops, etc, listing services rendered plus the correct amount of Italian VAT (IVA); they should be kept in case of checks by the Italian fiscal authorities.

OPENING TIMES

Generally, shops are open on week-

> ### Shopping
> Among the exquisite handicrafts of the region, the best souvenirs are ceramics from Albisola and Savona; hand-made lace in Portofino, Rapallo and Santa Margherita Ligure; macramé and woodcrafts from Chiavari; glass from Altare, where there is a glass-blowing centre.
>
> 'Made in Italy' is synonymous with style, and there are many opportunities for retail therapy in the specialist shops and designer emporia. For food delicacies, the olive oil is of extremely high quality, among the best in the whole country. The DOC wines are also a very good buy, especially the Cinque Terre wines and the highly prized Rossese.

days from 9am–7.30pm with a lunch break from 1–3.30pm. Many shops are closed on Saturday and Monday afternoons.

Banks are open from Monday to Friday between 8.30am and 1.30pm; some also open in the afternoon between 2.45pm and 3.45pm. Money can be exchanged at weekends in the railway stations and airports of the larger cities.

Museum opening hours vary considerably, and the times stated in this book are subject to change. State-owned museums are generally open daily from 9am–2pm, and 9am–1pm on Sunday and public holidays. They are often closed on Monday.

Note that some state-owned and municipal museums allow free admission to visitors under 18 and over 60 years of age.

Churches are usually closed around lunchtime, roughly from noon to 4pm.

PUBLIC HOLIDAYS

1 January: New Year's Day
6 January: Epiphany
Easter Sunday, Easter Monday
25 April: National Day of Liberation
1 May: Whit Sunday
15 August: Assumption of the Virgin *(ferragosto)*
1 November: All Saints
8 December: Immaculate Conception
25 and 26 December: Christmas

POSTAL SERVICES

Main post offices in major towns are open all day, otherwise the hours are 8am to 1.30pm. Stamps are sold at post offices and tobacconists.

TELEPHONE

You can call from public telephones using coins or with pre-paid phone cards *(carta telefonica)*, available for €2.50, €5 or €7.50 from many newsagents and tobacconists. It's a good idea to have both coins and a card handy. Bars and shops with a white and red phone sign in their windows also have public phones. If dialling from your hotel, check on the rate, which can be more than from public phone boxes.

Dialling codes from Italy: Australia 0061; United Kingdom 0044; US and Canada 001.

If calling within Italy, note that the area or city codes are dialled as part of the number even when calling within the same city or area. Thus a Genoa number always has the code 010 attached no matter where you're calling from. When calling from abroad, the 0 is always retained.

If using a US credit phone card, dial the company's access number: AT&T: 172-1011, Sprint: 172-1877, MCI: 172-1022.

TIME
Italy is six hours ahead of US Eastern Standard Time and one hour ahead of Greenwich Mean Time.

VOLTAGE
Usually 220v; occasionally 110v. Specialist electrical shops can provide the necessary adaptors.

Fire fighters at the ready.
In an emergency, dial 113

THEFT
To prevent theft, don't invite it in the first place: don't leave any valuables inside your car, always lock the vehicle when you leave it, and leave your cash in the hotel safe. When out walking in big towns and cities, keep a close eye on your camera and handbag (especially in the harbour section of Genoa).

MEDICAL
With Form E111 from the Department of Health and Social Security, UK visitors are entitled to reciprocal medical treatment in Italy. There are similar arrangements for other members of EU countries. It may nevertheless be advisable to take out insurance for private treatment in case of accident.

Holiday insurance policies and private patients schemes are recommended for non-EU visitors.

For minor ailments, chemists *(farmacia)* are well stocked with medicines, often sold without prescription.

EMERGENCIES
Public Emergency Assistance (fire, doctor, ambulance, police), tel: 113
Police Immediate Action, tel: 112
Breakdown service, tel: 116
Emergency medical assistance, tel: 118

ACCOMMODATION

With some 2,500 hotels and 180 camp-sites, the Italian Riviera has accommodation whatever your budget and tastes. Hotels are mostly at the resorts, and range from one (simple) to five (luxury) stars for comfort and service. Boarding houses *(pensione)* are plentiful, as are bed and breakfasts *(garni)*.

For July and August holidays, however, book well in advance; rooms in peak season are usually only available on half or full board.

In winter, many hotels in the coastal resorts are closed, while simpler establishments further inland are almost always open all year.

Brochures listing hotels in Liguria are available from Servizio Regionale di Promozione Turistica, Via Fieschi 15, I-16121 Genoa, tel: 010-548 4918, and from regional information offices.

Hotel Selection

Hotels are divided into price categories: €€€ = expensive, €€ = medium-priced and € = inexpensive.

Alassio

Beau Rivage, Via Roma,82, tel/fax: 0182 640585; closed 9 Oct– 25 Dec. Pleasant 19th-century villa overlooking the sea with simple but gracious rooms. 20 rooms. €€.

Grand Hotel Diana, Via Garibaldi 110, tel: 0182-642 701, fax: 0182-640 304; closed 6 Nov–6 Dec and 7 Jan–1 Feb. Terrace and shady garden plus indoor pool and private beach. Very comfortable hotel by the sea. Has facilities for the disabled. €€€.

Grand Hotel Spiaggia, Via Roma 78, tel: 0182-643 403, fax: 0182-640 279; closed 24 Oct–20 Dec. Sun terrace, pool and own beach make this perennially popular. 85 rooms. €€–€€€.

> **Prices and class**
> Hotels *(alberghi)* and boarding-houses *(pensioni)* are officially classed into five categories. However, this classification is based on amenities and services and does not reflect a qualitative assessment. Prices are set by the government and hotels should display them. Tax is usually included, but breakfast is generally not.

Albisola Capo

Park Hotel, Via Alba Docilia 3, tel/ fax: 019-482 355; 1½km (1 mile) south of Albisola Superiore. Only 11 rooms – but really pleasant and family run. €–€€.

Bordighera

Grand Hotel del Mare, Via Portico della Punta 34, tel: 0184-262 201, fax: 0184-262 394; closed 11 Oct–22 Dec. Hanging gardens, sea-water swimming pool and superb location make this a memorable hotel, catering for those who enjoy luxury. Situated about 2km (1 mile) east of Bordighera. €€€.
Villa Elisa, Via Romano 70, tel: 0184-261 313, fax: 0184-261 942; closed from 1 Nov– 20 Dec. Citrus and olive trees encircle the lovely garden and pool in the grounds of this comfortable villa; a popular choice. €€.

Camogli

Cenobio dei Dogi, Via Cuneo 34, tel: 0185-7241, fax: 0185-772 796. Patrician villa,built 1565, with all mod cons and pool-side terrace views. €€€.

Cinque Terre

Ca'd'Andrean, Manarola, Via Discovolo 101, tel: 0187-920 040, fax: 0187-920 452; closed 15 Nov–20 Dec. Comfortable hotel in an old oil-mill. Family run. €€.

Due Gemelli, Campi (4½km (3 miles) east of Riomaggiore), Via Litoranea 1, tel: 0187-920 678, fax: 0187-920 111. Beautiful site high above the sea, set in vineyards and chestnut groves. €.
Porto Roca, Monterosso al Mare, Via Corone 1, tel: 0187-817 502, fax: 0187-817 692. Right above the sea, with a superb view and private beach. €€–€€€.

Finale Ligure
Punta Est, Via Aurelia 1, tel: 019-600 611, fax: 600 611. Open Apr–mid-Oct. Comfortable 18th-century villa above sea. Exclusive but friendly. €€€.

Genoa
Agnello d'Oro, Via delle Monachette 6, tel: 010-246 2084, fax: 010-246 2327. Central location but quiet, dating from 17th century, with 35 rooms. €€.
La Capannina, Via Tito Speri 7, tel: 010-317 131, fax: 010-362 2692. Quiet and right by the sea in residential Albaro, near Boccadasse. €€.
Savoia Majestic, Via Arsenale di Terra 5, tel: 010-246 4132, fax: 010-261 883. Near Porta Principe station; modern comforts in a palatial hotel that has accommodated royalty. €€€.

Albergo on the coast:
not all hotels are open year round

Starhotel President, Corte Lambruschini 4, tel: 010-5727 fax: 010-553 1820. In the heart of Genoa, opposite the Brignole railway station, this is a modern and comfortable hotel. €€€.
Villa Pagoda, Via Capolungo 15, tel: 010-323200, fax: 010-321 218. Elegant villa, set in shady park €€€.

Imperia
Croce di Malta, Via Scarincio 148, tel: 0183-667 020, fax: 0183-63 687. Modern; by sea; harbour view. €€.

La Spezia
Firenze e Continentale, Via Paleocapa 7, tel: 0187-713 210, fax: 0187-714 930. In former old palazzo, pleasant, modern interior. Close to station. €€.
Genova, Via Fratelli Rosselli, 84, tel: 0187-732 972, fax: 0187-714 930; closed 24–27 Dec. Family-run, newly renovated and in town centre. Spacious lounges and entrance; simple rooms but pleasing, personalised décor. €€.

Lavagna
Giardini, Via Vinelli 9, tel: 0185-313 951, fax: 0185-323 096. Elegant and close to the cathedral. €€.
Villa Fieschi, Via Rezza 12, tel: 0185-304 400, fax: 0185-313 809; closed Nov–Feb. 13 rooms in lovely, old family-run villa in beautiful gardens. €€.

Noli

Ines, Via Vignolo 1, tel: 019-748 5428, fax: 019-748 086. Pleasant, family-run; 16 rooms; central. €–€€.

Miramare, Corso Italia 2, tel: 019-748 926, fax: 019-748 927; closed Nov. Enjoy a sense of history in this small hotel set in a 16th-century building a stone's throw from the sea. 28 rooms. €€.

> **Book ahead**
> Make sure you call or write before arriving to verify facilities and make reservations. Smaller hotels are not always cheaper; some of the more exclusive small hotels match the grand hotels in style and expense. But even inexpensive hotels offer basic comforts and good service.

Portofino

Eden, Via Dritto 20, tel: 0185-269 091, fax: 0185-269 047. Open in summer only. Central, just back from the port in a pretty two-storey villa with attractive gardens. 12 rooms. €–€€.

Piccolo Hotel, Via Duca degli Abruzzi 31, tel: 0185-269 015, fax: 0185-269 621; closed Nov–mid-Mar. Four-star establishment in a well-tended park, with a magnificent view of the Gulf from its balconies. €€€.

Portofino Kulm Hotel, Via Bernardo Gaggini 23, ruta di Camogli, tel: 0185-7361, fax: 0185-776 622 – about 30 mins drive from Portofino. Art nouveau, mountain-perched, newly restored little hotel. It has excited much interest for its lovely original detail and fabulous views towards France. €–€€.

Hotel Splendido, Viale Baratta 16, tel: 0185-267 801, fax: 0185-267 806; open Mar–Nov. Gorgeous villa located on the most 'chic' bay of the Riviera; this is where all the 'glitterati' still come to stay. A Portofino institution and very, very expensive. €€€.

Splendido Mare, Via Roma 2, tel: 0185-267 802, fax: 0185-267 807. Sister hotel to the 'Splendido', connected by a regular shuttle bus. Located on the main harbour square, the rooms are spacious and offer B&B rates, too. €€€.

Portovenere

Paradiso, Via Garibaldi 34–40, tel: 0187-790 612, fax: 0187-792 582. Pleasant atmosphere, magnificently situated with sea views. Rooms tend to be small. €€.

Rapallo

Astoria, Via Gramsci 4, tel: 0185-273 533, fax: 0185-62793. Art nouveau villa right next to the sea. €€–€€€.

Excelsior Palace Hotel, Via San Michele di Pagana 8, tel: 0185-230 666, fax: 0185-230 214. Elegant, beautifully appointed hotel overlooking the Gulf of Tigullio and Portofino. Every modern amenity, including health spa and conference facilities and excellent restaurant. €€€.

San Remo

Eveline-Portosole, Corso Cavallotti 111, tel: 0184-503 430, fax: 0184-503 431; closed 7–28 January. With just 22 rooms, this hotel has earned fame and favour over the past 50 years. Meticulous attention to detail and very romantic atmosphere – just a sigh away from the sea. No restaurant. €€–€€€.

Lolli Palace Hotel, Corso Imperatrice 70, tel: 0184-531 496, fax: 0184-541 574; closed 4 Nov–20 Dec. Traditional, family-run hotel, combining charm with excellent facilities. Lovely art nouveau building, with 51 rooms. €€.

Nazionale, Via Matteoti 3, tel: 0184-577 577, fax: 0184-541 612. Well placed for the Casino, this elegant hotel is still extremely popular and has been recently renovated. 78 rooms. €€€.

Royal, Corso Imperatrice 80, tel: 0184-5391, fax: 0184-661 445; closed 2 Oct–16 Dec. Established over a century ago: most luxurious in town. €€€.
Villa Mafalda, Corso Nuvoloni 18, tel: 0184-572 572, fax: 0184-572 574. Small, stylish, art-nouveau villa near casino; superb panoramic views; 34 rooms; no restaurant. €€–€€€.

Santa Margherita Ligure

Agriturismo Roberto Gnocchi, Via Romana 53, San Lorenzo della Costa (2½km (1½ miles) west of Santa Margherita Ligure), tel/fax: 0185- 283 431, open May–Oct. Must book. A stay here is like being a guest in a country house. Lovely sea views from terrace and gardens. 9 rooms. €€
Fasce, Via Bozzo 3, tel: 0185-286 435, fax: 0185-283 580; closed Jan–Feb. Well-run, family-owned hotel with 16 rooms; no restaurant. €–€€.
Grand Hotel Miramare, Lungomare Millite Ignoto 30, tel: 0185-287 013, fax: 0185-284 651. Beautiful, Liberty-style villa set in a flower-filled park. Every comfort and the beautiful location have made this one of the top hotels in the area. €€€.

Hotel Imperiale Palace,
five-star luxury in Santa Margherita

Hotel Continental, Via Pagana 8, tel: 0185-286 512, fax: 0185-284 463; closed 10 Jan–15 Feb. Grand, elegant, sea-front four-star hotel. Charming and attentive personal service by the Ciana family. Private beach. €€€.
Hotel Imperiale Palace, Via Pagana 19, tel: 0185-288 991, fax: 0185-284 223; open Easter–Oct. Five-star luxury hotel, elegant, historic and overlooking bay; with swiming pool. €€€.
Metropole, Via Pagana, 2, tel: 0185-286 134, fax: 0185-283 495, closed Nov. Set in floral park with sea views; traditional, elegant hotel and restaurant with Ligurian specialities. 59 rooms; four suites. Swimming pool. €€€.
Regina Elena, Lungomare Milite Ignoto 44, tel: 0185-287 003, fax: 0185-284 473 Also run by the Ciana family, this grand place has spectacular views over Tigullio Bay. Fully equipped health spa. €€€.
Tigullio et de Milan, Viale Rainusso 3, tel: 0185-287 455, fax. 0185-281 860. Close to the sea; modern hotel with 41 rooms set around a lovely garden. €€.

Savona

Mare, Via Nizza 89/r, tel: 019-264 065, fax: 019-263 277. Modern and elegant; right next to the sea, with a private beach. €€.

Sestri Levante
Due Mari, Vico del Coro 18, tel: 0185-42695, fax: 0185-42698; closed 24 Oct–23 Dec. The hotel is a refurbished 17th-century Genoese residence. Lovely gardens, swimming pool and private beach. €€.

Grand Hotel dei Castelli, Via alla Penisola 26, tel: 0185-487 020, fax: 0185-44767; open mid-Mar–beginning Nov. Medieval-style, grand building located on a scenic promontory. Lovely views over the sea and coast. €€€.

Grand Hotel Villa Balbi, Viale Rimembranza 1, tel: 0185-42941, fax: 0185-482459; closed 20 Oct–27 Dec. Three buildings in a park, of which the main is a spacious 17th-century villa with opulent furnishings. Open-air swimming pool and private beach. €€€.

Helvetia, Via Cappuccini 43, tel: 0185-41175, fax: 0185-457 216; closed Nov–Mar. Lovely terrace and flower garden overlooking the sea in the Baia del Silenzio ('Bay of Silence'). Private beach. 21 rooms; no restaurant. €€.

Triora
Colomba d'Oro, Corso Italia 66, tel: 0184-94051, fax: 0184-94089; open Apr–Oct. Friendly and clean, set in a former monastery; no televisions. €.

Varazze
Cristallo, Via Cilea 4, tel: 019-97264, fax: 019-935 5757; closed 20 Dec–6 Jan. A comfortable hotel with an attractive garden. 45 rooms with all facilities; use of the beach. €€.

Eden, Via Villagrande 1, tel: 019-932 888, fax: 019-96315. A modern, well-equipped hotel that is popular with both tourists and a business clientele. 45 rooms. €€.

Le Roi, Via Genova 43, tel: 019-95902, fax: 019-95903. Recently renovated small hotel with 16 rooms, facing the sea. Light and airy breakfast room with sea views. €€.

Ventimiglia
La Riserva di Castel d'Appio, Castel d'Appio 71, tel: 0184-229 533, fax: 0184-229 712; open Mar–Oct. Located about 5km (3 miles) outside Ventimiglia, this is a small establishment with a wonderful view of the Riviera dei Fiori and the Costa Azzurra (Côte d'Azur). All the rooms are comfortable and the service is courteous. €€.

Sole Mare, Via Marconi 22, tel: 0184-351 854, fax: 0184-230 988. Comfortable hotel enjoying a good location on the seafront, within easy distance of the centre. Pleasant garden. 28 rooms. €€.

YOUTH HOSTELS
There are four youth hostels along the Italian Riviera, but only two are open all year round: the Priamar hostel in Savona and the *Albergo per la Gioventù* in Genoa. The Wuillermin hostel in Finale and the Villa dei Franceschini in Savona are closed from mid-September to mid-March, and the Cristoforo Colombo in Genoa from 22 December to 22 January.

For more information on youth hostelling, contact the Associazione Italiana Alberghi per la Gioventù (AIG), Comitato Regionale, Salita Salvatore Viale 1/18, I-16128 Genoa, tel: 010-586 407.

Agriturismo
This is the Italian word for farm holidays, ideal for those keen on spending time close to nature. Families with children are finding these deals increasingly attractive, and *agriturismo* is an interesting alternative to the more 'usual' Riviera holiday. Farmers rent out rooms or apartments with varying standards of comfort, some reasonably priced and some expensive. For more information contact Agriturist Regionale, Via Invrea 11/10, I-16129 Genoa.

INDEX